D1236788

# AN ATLAS
# OF EXTINCT
# COUNTRIES

Gideon Defoe

# AN ATLAS
# OF EXTINCT
# COUNTRIES

Europa
*editions*

Europa Editions
1 Penn Plaza, Suite 6282
New York, N.Y. 10019
www.europaeditions.com
info@europaeditions.com

Library of Congress Cataloging in Publication Data is available
ISBN 978-1-60945-680-1

Defoe, Gideon
An Atlas of Extinct Countries

Book design by Emanuele Ragnisco
www.mekkanografici.com

Artwork © Joy Gosney 2020

Cover illustrations © Joy Gosney
Cover design layout © HarperCollinsPublishers Ltd 2020

Prepress by Grafica Punto Print—Rome

Printed in USA

# CONTENTS

For Elise

# AN ATLAS
# OF EXTINCT
# COUNTRIES

## GENEROUS TO A FAULT, THEY DIED DOING WHAT THEY LOVED: EXPORTING TIN

C ountries die. Sometimes it's murder. Sometimes it's an accident. Sometimes it's because they were too ludicrous to exist in the first place. Every so often they explode violently. A few slip away unnoticed. Often the cause of death is either "got too greedy" or "Napoleon turned up." Now and then they just hold a referendum and vote themselves out of existence.

These are the obituaries of the nations that fell off the map. The polite way of writing an obituary is: dwell on the good bits, gloss over the embarrassing stuff. A book about dead nations can't really do that, because it's impossible to skip the embarrassing stuff—there's far too much of it. The life stories of the sadly deceased involve a catalogue of chancers, racists, racist chancers, conmen, madmen, people trying to get out of paying taxes, mistakes, lies, stupid schemes and a lot of things that you'd file under the umbrella term of "general idiocy." Because of this—and because treating nation states with too much reverence is maybe the entire problem with pretty much everything—these accounts do not respectfully add to all the earnest flag-saluting in the world, however nice some of the flags are.

If you're sitting a boring geography exam, and want a book that sticks to a firm definition of what a country is, you are owed an apology.[1] You could write a very dry essay on all the failed attempts to define what counts as a "country," and if very dry essays are your thing then there are already a fair few out there. None of them get particularly close to an answer. There is something in biology called "the species problem." The problem being: after years of arguing about it, nobody can agree what criteria actually define a "species." Countries are no different. We switch definitions depending on whether we're at the United Nations, playing football, singing in Eurovision or buying cheese. It's a mess.

Having said that, here are some arbitrary rules: I've avoided delving too far into the past, because talking about ancient places as "nation states" is sort of meaningless when the idea itself didn't exist until the last few hundred years. I've ignored empires and colonies. I've left out places where the name has changed but the shape on the map has stayed the same. I've then immediately forgotten those rules by including Silla, Axum, New Caledonia and the Congo Free State. Please address angry letters about that to the UN Secretary-General. Or just pretend it's "in the tradition of Herodotus," which is a fancy way of saying that the story is more important than getting bogged down in endless caveats (caveat: caveats are good, and you should be rightfully suspicious of anything that tries to sum up the history of a place in 500 words).

If ex-nations seem unimportant in the big scheme of things then it's worth remembering that, like a Marvel superhero cash cow, countries don't always stay dead. Humans

[1] Another apology: a lot of these places are the stories of Posh White Guys, which is an unavoidable product of a time when only Posh White Guys felt entitled enough to go and set up countries.

live in a constant state of changing their minds about the type and number of other humans they want to be categorised with, so we oscillate from tiny blobs to huge empires and back again, and there's no reason to assume that process will ever stop. Within a decade, some of these geographical zombies might claw their way out of the graveyard and back into the atlas.

Please send hard currency in lieu of flowers. ALL HAIL NEUTRAL MORESNET.

A NOTE ON THE LOCATIONS: These maps use the what3words geocoding system. Instead of latitude and longitude, a set of three randomly assigned words can be used to uniquely identify the location of anything in the world, down to a resolution of three metres squared. One of the benefits of this is that it's much easier to remember three words than a string of numbers.

Visit what3words.com for more information.

# CHANCERS & CRACKPOTS

## The Kingdom of Sarawak
### 1841–1946

Population: between 8,000 (1841) and 600,000 (1946)
Capital: Kuching
Languages: English, Iban, Melanau, Bidayuh, Sarawak Malay, Chinese
Currency: Sarawak dollar
Cause of death: sold to the British
Today: part of Malaysia
///COMPOUND.MELONS.ORCHESTRA

While still a school kid, James Brooke declared his intention to run away to sea. He got as far as his gran's garden in Reigate. This combination of a lust for adventure, being slightly overdramatic and messing stuff up would be the main themes running through the rest of his life.

The KINGDOM of SARAWAK

SOUTH CHINA SEA

KUCHING

DUTCH BORNEO

No less determined to see the world by the time he was a teen, he joined the army, where his glorious military career ended as soon as it began. Charging into battle he was immediately shot, possibly in the lung, possibly somewhere significantly worse.[2]

After a painful recuperation, Brooke tried again. He already knew that his fabulously wealthy father was a soft touch, because when his brother had asked for an elephant, Brooke Senior obligingly had one shipped over at huge expense. James didn't want an elephant. He wanted a boat. Daddy obliged.

With his new toy, Brooke sailed for Borneo: the nineteenth-century poster child for savage, lush exoticism. The indigenous population, the Dayak, was divided into complicated rival factions, constantly skirmishing with each other, though mostly in the form of violent dance-offs. Brooke successfully played the competing groups against each other—taking the side of the "land dayaks," rather than the piratical "sea dayaks" (a terminology that he invented). Bringing a measure of order to the local chaos, he was awarded a chunk of territory by a grateful Sultan of Brunei, who had wrongly assumed that Brooke, very much a private citizen chancer, somehow represented the British Empire. He was also given a pet orangutan called Betsy.

Aged just 38, he had his own kingdom. "I am really becoming a great man, dearest mother," Brooke wrote in a letter home, displaying all the modest self-effacement that rich English Victorian white dudes are generally famous for. But in an era of greedy Brits abroad, Brooke only registers as about a five-out-of-ten on the Imperialistic Git scale. He seems to have genuinely wanted the best for "his people," albeit in the patro-

---

[2] Probably lies: it seems likely that, in an era when homosexuality was punishable by death, the rumour that Brooke had been shot through the penis was just a neat way to explain away his perpetual bachelordom.

nising paternalistic way of the time. He set up a court of justice to bring law to his new domain, and famously sentenced a man-eating crocodile to death (because, though he respected and sympathised with the animal, he didn't want the other crocodiles to get the wrong idea about what was "acceptable behaviour.") The local Dayak population were keen headhunters,[3] an activity Brooke tried semi-successfully to discourage—and however much of a cultural relativist you are, that's probably not the worst thing in the world.

At first, Brooke became a national hero back in Britain. But in a rare bit of imperial navel-gazing, some wondered if swanning off and starting your own kingdom was perhaps a Bit Much. Political enemies accused him of massacring innocents. Brooke claimed they were pirates. There was an enquiry, which in the usual style of government enquiries quickly got bogged down in weird little details, such as trying to define what a pirate was. Did pirates have to have sails? What if they just had paddles? Predictably, nothing came of it.

Sarawak slid into debt, and Brooke's local crush[4] was killed during a Chinese insurrection. He became increasingly depressed and hoped the United Kingdom would buy the country off him, but they weren't keen. So the rule of the "White Rajahs" bumbled on, with the title passing to Brooke's nephew, Charles, who did a pretty decent job of getting the place back on its feet, and whose most distinguishing feature was a glass eye (purchased at a taxidermist's and intended for an albatross—though one rumour suggested that he had a

---

[3] The Dayaks viewed headhunting as means of consecrating important events. It was considered extremely bad luck not to give a human skull to your wife at the birth of your child.

[4] James Brooke seems to have fallen for the local rajah's brother, Badrudeen, and wrote a lot of torturously evasive diary entries about him.

range of different fake eyes from different creatures, to wear according to his mood). Charles was succeeded by his son Vyner. Vyner had a difficult time of it. He had been forbidden from eating jam as a child because his dad deemed it "effeminate" and grew up so socially anxious that he would hide from guests in a cupboard. Hiding in a cupboard wasn't going to be enough to avoid World War II and the Japanese invasion that came with it. Vyner fled to Australia. Once the war was over he briefly regained his kingdom, only to find it bombed to bits. With nothing left in the Sarawak coffers to rebuild, Vyner faced up to the inevitable. He finally persuaded the British to take it off his hands in exchange for a big lump of cash and all the jam he could eat.

# THE KINGDOM OF BAVARIA
## 1805–1918

POPULATION: CIRCA 6.5 MILLION (1910)
CAPITAL: MUNICH
LANGUAGES: BAVARIAN, UPPER GERMAN
CURRENCY: BAVARIAN GULDEN, GERMAN GOLDMARK
CAUSE OF DEATH: BAD GENES AND BISMARCK
TODAY: PART OF GERMANY
///SUBTEXTS.PHOTOS.DIETARY

Every morning, Ludwig II, the fourth king of Bavaria, would have his barber tease out his hair into a weird bouffant that made his head look massive. He claimed that without his daily coiffure he could not enjoy his food. If a servant happened to accidentally stare at him and his big hair for too long, Ludwig would empty a washbasin over them. That's what a few hundred years of royal inbreeding gets you.

The KINGDOM of BAVARIA

BAYREUTH

BOHEMIA

MUNICH

SWITZERLAND

AUSTRIA

Bavaria existed as part of the Holy Roman Empire for centuries, but it was only after Napoleon steamrollered Austria in 1805 that it became a kingdom. The relatively normal King Maximilian helped defeat the French and managed to expand the country's borders as a reward for his troubles. Maximilian was followed by his son Ludwig. Ludwig I was both a patron of the arts and a notorious lothario[5] (he commissioned a series of portraits of "famous beauties of the day") but the old letch (61) met his match in Lola Montez (28). An Irish dancer posing as an exotic Andalusian, Lola had already barrelled through Europe, leaving chaos in her wake. She'd caused a riot in Warsaw, shocked high society in Paris, and had a scrape with the cops in Berlin. When she arrived in Munich she shacked up with Ludwig and persuaded him to liberalise the place, which didn't win him many friends among the ultra-conservative Catholic aristocracy. At the same time, revolutionary fervour swept through Europe in 1848, and Ludwig, besieged from all sides, decided to abdicate, correctly guessing that a nice retirement pottering around his garden would be a lot more fun than being a head of state.[6]

His son, Maximilian II, valiantly tried to keep the kingdom from getting hoovered up by Otto von Bismarck, who was now embarked upon his grand project to unify Germany under a dominant Prussia. But the new king inconveniently died young in 1864, which brought on the reign of Ludwig II and his big hair. It's unfair to say that Ludwig wasn't interested in ruling Bavaria—he worked quite hard at the job—but it certainly

[5] Ludwig I's wedding was the first Oktoberfest. Bavaria would later make the adoption of its beer purity law a condition of joining the German Empire.

[6] After her stint in Bavaria, Lola headed to California where appreciative miners would supposedly throw gold nuggets at her.

wasn't where his heart lay. That was with opera. More specifi-
cally, the operas of genius/all-round horrible anti-Semite
Richard Wagner. Ludwig was Wagner's number-one fan. He
built his idol a world-famous opera house. He wrote stacks of
letters to the composer, none of which contain a single joke.
He almost bankrupted himself constructing over-the-top fairy-
tale castles (sketched out by Wagner's stage designer).
Contemporary wags started referring to Wagner as "Lola
Two." Faced with the task of having to juggle loyalties to wily
Bismarck and the Austrians, all Ludwig wanted to do was run
away with his pal to Switzerland. He backed the wrong side in
the Austro-Prussian War, and by 1870 had been forced, distracted by toothache, to join victorious Prussia's North
German Confederation.[7] He at least managed to maintain a
degree of independence for his kingdom—they kept their own
army, railways and postal service, and he could go on building
his fantastically camp castles.

The strain of trying to navigate Bavaria's path through the
tangled politics of the times started to show. The revisionist
take is that Ludwig wasn't mad in any medically recognised
way, but that his doctors plotted with political enemies to label
him as such. It's impossible to say, though nobody disputes
that he became troublingly erratic and, if not mad, then certainly a bit of a dick. He took to ordering people to be exe-
cuted for sneezing (orders which were quietly ignored). At one
point he tried to hire bandits in a bizarre scheme to capture the
Prussian crown prince and have him "chained up in a cave."
He'd organise expensive performances of plays for which he
was the only audience member.[8]

---

[7] Bismarck did not endear himself to the Bavarians when he described
them as "half-way between an Austrian and a human being."

[8] Ludwig II tried to go on holiday with an actor friend, but his efforts to
travel incognito were messed up when a boat he hired in Lucerne turned up
decked out in Bavarian flags and the captain greeted him as "your majesty."

Concerned ministers or political rivals (depending on who you ask) decided enough was enough and took him away to be "cured." Locked in the grounds of Berg Castle, Ludwig went for an evening walk with his physician. The bodies of both men were found a little later floating in the nearby lake. Whether misadventure or suicide or good old-fashioned murder, the kingdom wouldn't recover. The title officially passed to Ludwig's brother Otto at first, but he was *definitely* insane, and so his uncle Luitpold ruled as regent. For the next few years Bavaria passively slipped further and further into the clutches of the German Empire, almost without anyone noticing. It was an oddly underwhelming end for such a headline-grabbing dynasty.

# THE ISLANDS OF REFRESHMENT
## 1811–16

POPULATION: 4
CAUSE OF DEATH: A BOATING ACCIDENT
TODAY: A BRITISH OVERSEAS TERRITORY
///UNTIRING.CRANES.SKIMMED

Today there is a sign on Tristan da Cunha welcoming visitors to "the Remotest Island." 1,500 miles from anywhere, this isn't tourist-board hyperbole. The Portuguese explorer Tristão da Cunha spotted the tiny volcanic speck in 1506, but decided it looked too unappealing to stop off at. It wasn't until 1811 that the first would-be permanent settler showed up, a young adventurer from Salem, Massachusetts, named Jonathan Lambert.[9]

---

[9] Probably lies: Lambert thought he was the first person to ever stay on the island, but the presence of pigs suggests other people, probably Dutch traders, must have stopped off first, at least briefly.

He'd hitched a lift on a whaling ship, along with a dog and three companions. One of these, Thomas Currie, had been promised 12 Spanish dollars a month to help set up a new country. They rowed ashore and Lambert boldly announced the land as his own, "solely for myself and my heirs for ever." He instantly embarked on a rebranding exercise, collectively rechristening da Cunha and its two equally windswept neighbours ("Nightingale" and "Inaccessible") with a more approachable-sounding name—the Islands of Refreshment. This welcoming kingdom had the stated aim of providing refreshment to passing travellers—"all vessels, of whatever description, and belonging to whatever nation, will visit me for that purpose." Lambert had, in effect, set up a glorified motorway service station, but in the stupidest place possible: an obscure part of the Atlantic where the only passing ships, far from civilisation as they could be, were inclined to nick stuff rather than pay for it.[10]

Just like a real motorway services, things were bleak. The new inhabitants butchered an enormous number of seals, hoping to make enough oil from the blubber to sell to passing mariners to pay for a nicer boat. They ate a lot of turnips, their only substitute for bread. Life proved difficult. Then, in 1812, one year into the project, Lambert and two others disappeared: presumed drowned in a boating accident while out fishing. Thomas Currie—seething about never having been paid by his vanished boss—was left to fend for himself.

It was a grumpy Currie who recounted the whole sorry escapade to the British when they turned up four years later. They'd come to claim the island as a naval base, worried it might otherwise be used as a stopping-off point from which to mount a rescue of Napoleon, newly exiled on St. Helena. It

[10] Today, it is still a six-day boat journey from the nearest mainland, South Africa.

seems like precautionary overkill, because St. Helena is still 1,343 miles away, but they'd learned their lesson from the whole Elba fiasco (*see* page 86).

Swallowed by the British Empire, the independent Islands of Refreshment were no more, but this new occupation finally led to a slightly more successful community getting established there. Nowadays they even have a British postcode.[11] Though they also have several cases of progressive blindness caused by retinitis pigmentosa, because Tristan da Cunha has become an unfortunate case study in why tiny gene pools are Not A Great Thing.

---

[11] Evacuated to Hampshire in 1961 after a volcanic eruption, virtually the entire population voted to return to the island, so it can't be as bad as Currie made out.

THE KINGDOM OF CORSICA
MARCH–NOVEMBER 1736

CAPITAL: CERVIONE
LANGUAGES: ITALIAN, CORSICAN, FRENCH, GERMAN
CURRENCY: SOLDI
CAUSE OF DEATH: IN-FIGHTING AND BAD DEBTS
TODAY: PART OF FRANCE
///AUCTIONING.POLITICIANS.FATTEN

Theodore Stephan Freiherr von Neuhoff—of "fine form and a handsome face"—left a trail of debts, inspired an opera and a couple of novels, got punched by jealous husbands, and basically did all the eighteenth-century Errol Flynn stuff you could hope for.

KINGDOM
OF
SARDINIA

REPUBLIC OF GENOA

LIGURIAN SEA

The
KINGDOM of
CORSICA

ELBA

CERVIONE

Born into a semi-noble family in Cologne, he joined the army at 17, where he started a lifelong habit of racking up huge gambling losses.[12] Then he did a runner across Europe, marrying one of the Queen of Spain's maids en route. Whose jewellery he then stole, before heading back to Paris where he used the swag to invest in one of the first financial bubbles.[13]

Aged 26, bankrupt and living in south London, von Neuhoff hid in bed to avoid his creditors, read books about highwaymen and got heavily into alchemy. He quit England and headed back to the continent, where he had an affair with a nun. The only thing more illegal than having an affair with a nun was working as a "magicotherapist," so he did that too, telling people he could predict lottery numbers, exorcise demons and make love potions.[14] While plying this slippery trade in Genoa, he encountered some Corsican rebels. The rebels were after self-determination, free from the yoke of the Genoese. Everyone hated Genoa by this point in history, and the Corsicans had a legitimate grievance—they were regarded as "barbarians" by their rulers, and forbidden from hunting or fishing.[15] Partly attracted by the romance of helping the plucky underdog, mostly attracted to the opportunity of smuggling coral, Theodore agreed to help them, on the proviso that, should this all work out, he be declared king. He borrowed money—borrowing money being his main skill—and purchased arms for

---

[12] Theodore would try to pay off his creditors with promissory notes which, when opened, turned out to be blank bits of paper.

[13] The Mississippi scheme was the brainchild of John Law, a Scottish banker who invented most of the traits of bankers we still know and love—ruinous financial products, rampant speculation and a ridiculous property bubble that almost ruined France.

[14] Other jobs attempted by Theodore: "virtuoso," "language teacher" and "connoisseur of pictures." During his magicotherapist years he went by the name "Baron von Syburg."

[15] One person who later tried to defend Genoa's treatment of the Corsicans was Mussolini, which is not much of an endorsement.

the cause. He sought alliances in Turkey and Morocco but, sympathetic as they were, nobody wanted to get involved. So, he returned to Corsica—decked out in his new king outfit (fur-trimmed robe, plumed tricorn, gilded cane) and—either by luck or unexpected military skill—drove the Genoese back to a couple of fortified enclaves.

Theodore then issued a set of articles: there would be low taxes, he would found a university and no foreigners could be king (apart from him). He got rid of the unpopular *attacar* custom, which dictated that a man who touched or was seen alone with a woman was required to marry her, regardless of either party's feelings on the matter. After a good harvest, Corsica improbably found itself doing better under its dubious king than anyone had the right to expect.

But the island famous for its vendettas was never going to be an easy place to run.[16] One of the Corsican rebels in particular, Giacinthio Paoli, had it in for Theodore. By nature liberal, and always with one eye on the financial side of things, Theodore had proclaimed religious tolerance of Jews—which was a step too far for Paoli and the conservative Corsicans. When the Genoese posted up notices telling the islanders about their king's iffy past, Paoli happily stoked the rumours and discontent. Theodore was forced to flee, first to Florence and eventually to Amsterdam, still trying to raise the funds he needed to secure his kingdom.

In an Amsterdam pub, one of his creditors recognised him and Theodore's luck ran out. He ignobly offered his kingdom to Spain if they'd pay his debt for him, but Spain refused. Thrown into a debtor's jail,[17] but a huckster to the end, he still

[16] Corsica today has the highest per capita murder rate in Europe.

[17] Later in life, incarcerated in England, Theodore successfully campaigned to have a nicer prison built. He died in Soho, aged 62.

managed to produce a prospectus trying to lure investors with lucrative-sounding tales of Corsica's olive oil, almonds and figs, despite the obvious lost cause of the whole enterprise. If he had been alive today, he would almost certainly be raising venture capital millions for pointless juicers.

# THE STATE OF MUSKOGEE
## 1799–1803

POPULATION: CIRCA 50,000
CAPITAL: MIKASUKE
LANGUAGES: ENGLISH, VARIOUS MUSKOGEAN
CAUSE OF DEATH: A DOUBLE CROSS
TODAY: PART OF FLORIDA, USA
///LIVE.BURSTING.SMOKE

In the eighteenth century, William Bowles, a bored 14-year-old in the Maryland, joined a Loyalist regiment fighting on the side of the British in the American War of Independence. He found the military even duller than his previous life, and fast became "stir crazy and insubordinate." Before long, his commanding officers had had enough of Bowles turning up late to everything and kicked him out, so he ran away to live with the Native Americans. He wasn't unique in this—hundreds of white men threw in their lot with the locals—but he was unique in the size of his dreams.

The STATE of
MUSKOGEE

MIKASUKE

FLORIDA

Bowles envisaged "an entirely new nation state rising up out of the swamps" under the leadership of—don't drop your monocle in shock at this—William Bowles. It would be called Muskogee, after the Muscogee (or Creek) people, and it would be a self-governing "Indian nation," right where what is now Florida starts to droop into the Gulf of Mexico. Here the indigenous Creek and Cherokee would live free from both the Spanish (currently in charge) and the Americans (looming ominously). The way the country would maintain this unlikely independence was by pledging loyalty to the British Empire, who would help defend it should the need arise. Note: if your plan involves the British coming to your rescue at any point, then it is a Bad Plan. Can't emphasise this enough.

Nonetheless, Bowles left his Creek wife and headed off on a sort of glad-handing tour, trying to secure aid for the project. He went to Nova Scotia and the Bahamas and Quebec and finally London, where he petitioned George III (not yet loopy), introducing himself as "the leader of an independent and populous nation."[18] The British gave a shrug and some vague words of tacit approval. Satisfied, Bowles got to work on designing a flag, because these types always jump straight to that. Flag and motto hammered out—"Liberty or death!"—in 1792 he sailed into New Orleans, looking to sit down with the Spanish and come to an agreement that would avoid war. The Spanish governor listened hard and nodded along and suggested that it all sounded fine but advised Bowles that he should head over to Cuba to speak to some slightly higher-up authorities. Just to rubberstamp everything.

It was a trap. As soon as Bowles showed up in Cuba, the Spanish clapped him in irons and shipped him off to Cádiz.

---

[18] The title William Bowles awarded himself was "Director General and Commander-In-Chief of the Muskogee Nation."

From there they shipped him another few thousand miles away to the Philippines—far enough, they felt, to be permanently out of their hair. Bowles wasn't to be put off so easily. He borrowed a tenner and made his way to London, then booked passage back to America, where, in 1800, he tried it all again.

Bowles and 300 Creek warriors seized a Spanish fort and hoisted his flag. Near to present-day Tallahassee, he began building his capital. He unveiled bold plans to start a newspaper and a university. But news of a truce between Britain and Spain, coupled with growing doubts about the flamboyant Bowles's skill as a statesman, meant the Creek had already lost faith in their would-be leader. They struck a deal behind his back: in exchange for debt forgiveness, they would turn him over to the Spanish once again.

For the second time, Bowles found himself a prisoner in Havana. This time there wouldn't be an escape—refusing to eat, because he was understandably pretty fed up by this point, Bowles wasted away. The Creek fared no better without him— the United States would soon swoop into Muscogee territory. The town Bowles had built, and the nation he had tried to lead, were all but wiped out by genocidal future-president Andrew Jackson, who got himself put on the twenty-dollar bill for his troubles.

# THE REPUBLIC OF SONORA
## 1853–4

CAPITAL: LA PAZ
CAUSE OF DEATH: NOBODY TOOK IT SERIOUSLY
TODAY: PART OF MEXICO
///BETRAYED.PLUNGE.DEBATING

By 1848 the United States seemed to have stopped growing, and that annoyed a lot of people. Continual expansion—"Manifest Destiny"—was regarded as a God-given right. If the government wasn't up to the task, then it was down to individuals with the Right Stuff, individuals who would take that Manifest Destiny into their own strong, patriotic hands. This was the age of the filibusters, back when the term still referred to plundering adventurers rather than politicians talking for ages. Enter William Walker—five foot two, pale and slight, "as unprepossessing-looking a person as one would meet in a day's walk."

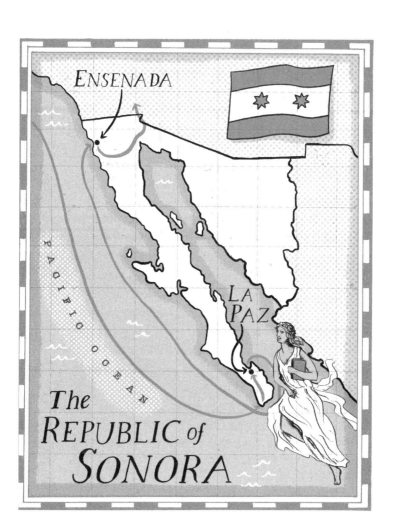

Walker had already studied medicine and law[19] and watched his fiancée die of yellow fever by the time he moved out west to San Francisco, where he managed to get sent to jail for writing an article criticising a local judge. He became briefly famous for a duel in which he was shot twice because he'd never used a revolver before and didn't know how to work it properly. Not letting any of that dampen his spirits, he travelled to the Mexican-controlled region of Sonora, where he approached the government with a simple request: he wanted to turn the place into an American colony. A lot of Mexicans had headed north to work in California, Walker pointed out, and the land was now vulnerable to attack from the Apache. It would be in Mexico's best interests for him to take over. Mexico unsurprisingly failed to follow his logic and turned him down. Without missing a beat, Walker returned to San Francisco where he set about selling bonds for his proposed new nation and started to raise an army. Men who had failed to strike lucky in the gold rush eagerly signed up, promised land rich in silver as a reward.

Walker's tiny army, 50 or so strong, successfully seized the city of La Paz in Baja California. The eagle-eyed might note that La Paz is still a few hundred miles away from Sonora, but that didn't stop Walker proclaiming it "a great victory." Back in San Francisco, they went nuts for this news. Walker declared all of Baja California his, which was bold, if a bit meaningless.[20] The Mexicans attacked his new "capital" in Ensenada but were held back. Unfortunately, at about this point Walker's only boat sailed off unexpectedly (the captain

[19] Having grown up an obvious prodigy in Nashville, Tennessee, Walker—who liked to get about—attended both the University of Edinburgh and the University of Heidelberg.

[20] A newspaper of the day idly wondered why Walker didn't save himself a lot of bother and simply claim to have conquered the whole of Mexico while he was busy claiming things.

possibly bribed by the prisoners on board) and he was left without any supplies. An already semi-farcical situation had become really farcical, but Walker took no notice whatsoever. He pressed on towards the east, and—again having barely done anything in terms of actual conquering—proclaimed the land successfully annexed, christened it the Republic of Sonora and named himself president.

Illness, desertions and bandits quickly reduced his very small army into a band of about 30. Even for someone with the Tom Cruise-like level of self-belief displayed by Walker, it was pretty obvious that you couldn't seriously be considered to be running a country with a force of 30. He reluctantly trudged his men to the relative safety of the American fort at San Diego. They arrested him, because setting up countries in direct contravention of international treaties is fairly illegal. But at his trial, in the spirit of the time, it took a jury just eight minutes to acquit him.

It might have been a kindness if they hadn't. Walker had gotten a taste for filibustering, and would later try the exact same trick in Nicaragua,[21] where he once again managed to become president/mess up/get captured/be sent back to the United States/get put on trial/have a jury instantly acquit him. A lesser/more sensible man would have called that a day. Not Walker. His final, fatal attempt to do it all for a *third* time saw him come unstuck in Honduras. This time though, when it all went wrong, Walker wound up facing a Honduran firing squad rather than an American jury. He was still only 36.

[21] After a military defeat in Rivas, Nicaragua, he deliberately contaminated the local water wells with corpses, causing a cholera epidemic that killed thousands.

## The Kingdom of Araucanía & Patagonia
### 1860–62

CAPITAL: PERQUENCO (HYPOTHETICALLY)
LANGUAGE: MAPUDUNGU (HYPOTHETICALLY)
CAUSE OF DEATH: WOULD-BE KING DECLARED A LUNATIC
TODAY: PART OF CHILE
///STARGAZING.SHOPKEEPERS.FLOGGING

The indigenous Mapuche peoples of South America hadn't been treated well by new arrivals to their lands—a sentence so predictable it's almost not worth typing. They had done their best to hold off first the Incas and then the Spanish, but the establishment of an independent Chile in the middle of the nineteenth century proved disastrous for them. The Mapuche found themselves displaced and stateless. What they needed was a wily French lawyer. At least, that's what wily French lawyer Orélie-Antoine de Tounens decided they needed. A wily French lawyer who could also be their king.

In 1858 de Tounens read a sixteenth-century epic poem about the conquest of Chile and liked it so much he decided to borrow 25,000 francs and set sail for a new life in the Andes.[22] He arrived at Coquimbo, a bustling port clinging to rocky hills, and set about learning Spanish. He bought himself a poncho to complement a look which was already very "failed magician." After a couple of years hanging around the neighbourhood, he managed to arrange a meeting with a group of Mapuche tribal leaders. The deal he proposed was simple: Chile had no legal claim on the Mapuche territory. He would argue their case, help them find arms and win the French over to their side. In return, he would be elected Great Toqui, Supreme Chieftain of the Mapuches. It's not totally clear to what extent the locals went along with this, but before long de Tounens had issued a decree, published in the Chilean newspapers. It announced Araucanía and Patagonia as an independent state.

He'd assumed that the French, who were rapidly losing their empire, would be interested in helping this new potential ally gain a foothold in the continent. They weren't. When de Tounens tried to raise an army, the Chilean forces captured him. He was thrown in jail, and then a lunatic asylum. The French consulate managed to secure his release and he was shipped back home.

A Parisian court decided that his claims to the kingdom were bogus and agreed with Chile that de Tounens was mad. Royal decrees signed by non-existent ministers named "the chair" didn't help his case. De Tounens refused to give up, established an Araucanían newspaper—*The Steel Crown*—and soon attempted to return to his kingdom. Despite his fake

---

[22] De Tounens had big plans right from the start. "Forced to choose a career," he wrote, "I quickly made up my mind to study law, with the sole objective of preparing myself for my future endeavours as a king.'

passport, the Chilean authorities instantly recognised him. They deported him for a second time. On his final attempt at venturing to Araucanía he wound up getting robbed, was captured again and fell gravely ill, forcing him back to France once more.

Back in 1872, de Tounens had placed an advert announcing that he was seeking a bride—"a maid who would be willing to share my destiny . . . so that I might sire an heir." This smooth line didn't work, so after he died, miserable and still unrecognised as a legitimate king, his heir ended up being a random champagne salesman he had met on his travels. The crown of Araucanía has since changed hands down the years, and while Orélie's "successors" continue to squabble over a non-existent title, the Mapuche are still fighting for their land and their rights. Given that the rest of us are very into our mobile phones and there's a lot of lithium buried in those ancestral lands, the odds are not on their side.

# The Heavenly Kingdom of Great Peace
## 1851–64

POPULATION: 30 MILLION (AT GREATEST EXTENT)
CAPITAL: TIANJING (PRESENT DAY NANJING)
CURRENCY: "SHENGBAO" COINAGE
CAUSE OF DEATH: AN UNRELIABLE PROPHET
TODAY: PART OF CHINA
///PINKS.HOURGLASS.BINS

In 1964, Pepsi ditched "The Sociables Prefer Pepsi" as a slogan in favour of the slicker "Come alive! You're in the Pepsi generation!" When they exported this marketing campaign to China, their ad agency mistranslated it as the bold but misleading "Pepsi brings your ancestors back from the grave." Even if this story is not as apocryphal as it sounds, it is very much not the worst case of things getting lost in translation between the East and West. For that, you need to go back to the first half of the nineteenth century, and a mistake that led to the deadliest civil war in history.

The HEAVENLY KINGDOM of GREAT PEACE

TIANJING

CHINA

Hong Xiuquan was desperate to become a civil servant, but to do so he had to travel to the big city and pass an exam. He failed the first time. The second time he failed again, but on his way out of the exam someone handed him a Christian pamphlet: a slightly garbled translation of the Bible's greatest hits, with added demons. Hong didn't read the tract particularly thoroughly, but on the contents page he saw a symbol he recognised: the Chinese character for his own name. In a cosmic bit of bad luck *hong* means "flood," and he noted that his namesake "destroyed every living thing upon the Earth."

When he failed his exam for the third time, Hong had what today we'd probably recognise as a total nervous breakdown. He took to bed with a feverish vision, in which a bearded man gave him a sword. Reading through the pamphlet once again, confused chunks of his dream and the biblical tales tumbled together. The upshot was that Hong skipped a few logical steps and concluded that he must be the Chinese younger brother of Jesus, and that his mission was to rid the world of demons.

Word spread quickly through a febrile populace,[23] and a devoted cult grew up around Hong, known as the God Worshippers. Mao would later airbrush out the more bonkers religious component and celebrate the movement as the first workers' uprising, which to an extent is what it was.[24] The "demons" Hong believed he had to vanquish took the form of the oppressive Qing dynasty. Convinced of his destiny, Hong and his army managed to win a series of ever more bloody battles, culminating in the capture of the city of

[23] An important context is that the First Opium War with the drug-pushing British had left China on the edge by this point.

[24] Hong's teachings included equality of the sexes (though they had to be segregated) and for the people to pool their resources, which is the bit Mao picked up on.

Nanjing, where he established the capital of his Heavenly Kingdom of Great Peace.

But the Qing fought back. Gradually, Hong's God Worshippers found themselves on the losing side of what had become "total war," with everything and everywhere a target.[25] By 1864, the enemy had the Heavenly Capital entirely surrounded. The fighting headed underground—Qing forces dug tunnels to get past the city's impenetrable walls, while the God Worshippers dug counter-tunnels, flooding the enemy tunnels with sewage. Inside the blockaded city, starvation loomed. But Hong, serenely unperturbed, told his followers not to worry—instead of food they could eat "manna." He never bothered to define the exact nature of this magical substance, but he himself took to eating old weeds from the palace grounds. Before very long he fell unsurprisingly ill, because rotten vegetation will do that. Twenty days later, he died.

Soon after Hong's death, the Qing general Zeng Guoquan set off a series of explosions deep in the tunnels, and the walls of Nanjing fell. To really make their point, in a pretty literal definition of overkill, the victorious Qing exhumed Hong's body, beheaded him, burned the corpse and, finally, shot the ashes out of a cannon. Even Jesus's younger brother couldn't come back from that.[26]

---

[25] Estimates of the number of dead are all over the place, but the most conservative guess puts it at 20 million. It might have been as many as 100 million.

[26] Though it took another seven years after Hong's death for the last vestiges of the God Worshippers to be wiped out.

# Rapa Nui (Easter Island)
## circa 1200–1888

POPULATION: 12,000 (AT MAXIMUM)

CAPITAL: NOT A "CAPITAL" AS SUCH, BUT HANGA ROA IS THE
MAIN BAY

LANGUAGE: RAPA NUI

CAUSE OF DEATH: A COMBINATION OF RATS, DISEASE, NOT
THINKING THINGS THROUGH, GODAWFUL EUROPEANS

TODAY: PART OF CHILE

///IDENTIFICATION.REPAYS.RATS

In 1866, a boat arrived at Easter Island with two missionaries on board. Unfortunately, also on board: former arms dealer and all-round murderous psychopath Jean-Baptiste Dutrou-Bornier. Within 12 years he would have proclaimed himself king, wiped out most of the population and turned the entire island into a sheep ranch.

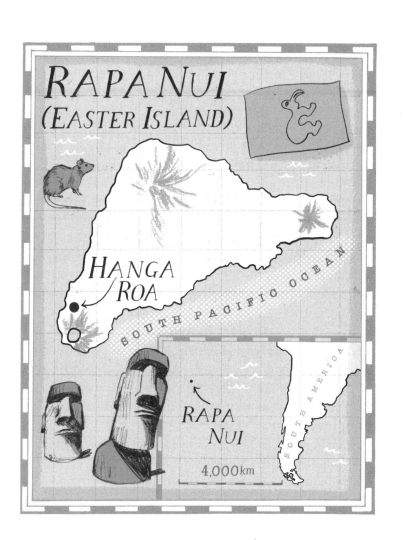

RAPA NUI
(EASTER ISLAND)

HANGA ROA

SOUTH PACIFIC OCEAN

RAPA NUI

SOUTH AMERICA

4,000km

The origin myths of the indigenous Rapa Nui people tell of a primeval being called Makemake who failed to have sex with first a gourd, then a stone, but got lucky with a mound of soil, out of which emerged a human. Radiocarbon dating and mitochondrial DNA suggest a more recent Polynesian origin for the Rapa Nui, who seem to have emigrated to the island about 800 years ago. These first settlers soon settled down into two warring clans: the Tu'u to the west and the 'Oto 'Itu to the east. Each clan erected their own examples of the famous giant-headed *moai* sculptures, and then did their best to knock the other side's efforts down.[27] Even when stuck in the middle of the ocean, humans will still find a way to disagree with approximately 50 per cent of their neighbours over some stupid thing.

Of course, the other skill humans are good at is ruining the environment, so the Rapa Nui set about doing that too. They cut down trees at a prodigious rate. Which they might have gotten away with, but they'd accidentally imported the Polynesian rat with them. The rats gobbled all the Jubaea nuts that would have provided new palm trees. Grass replaced wood as fuel, the population declined, the seabirds vanished, Eden became a desert.[28] This was a relative golden time compared to what came next.

In the nineteenth century, traders from Peru started to target the islanders, capturing an estimated half of the population. Tuberculosis and smallpox added to their woes. The Brits nicked a couple of sacred statues. Then the missionaries turned up, and the captain of their boat, Dutrou-Bornier. With a megalomaniacal zeal, he set about terrorising the place. First,

[27] "El Gigante" is an unfinished moai statue that would have been over 20 metres tall if the islanders had ever been able to stand it up.

[28] Though some recent archaeological research posits that the Rapa Nui culture made a better fist of things than previously supposed, prior to the arrival of Europeans.

he dabbled in his own bit of slave trading. Then he started buying up the island, piece by piece. He hoisted his own flag. He kidnapped local women—one of whom, Koreto, he took as a "wife." On sales receipts for the land he was supposedly purchasing, she was recorded as "the Queen of Easter Island."

When the missionaries tried to stop him, he attacked them. The islanders wrote a letter to the bishop of Tahiti requesting help, the first time they had ever sought outside assistance. The bishop asked the French navy to step in. They didn't bother. The missionaries fled with as many islanders as could fit on their boat. Dutrou-Bornier set about building his sheep ranch.

In the end, the few remaining Rapa Nui took matters into their own hands. A small group ambushed and murdered Dutrou-Bornier,[29] but the damage had already been done. By the time of his death there were only 110 people left, 26 of them women. Not long after that, Chile—a country 2,000 miles away, with no Polynesian population—decided to stake their dubious claim. They employed an age-old contractual trick: the Chilean version of the paperwork made it clear that the island would become part of the territory of Chile. The Rapa Nui version simply referred to their being "a friend of the island."

---

[29] The specific event that supposedly led to Dutrou-Bornier's murder was an argument about the poor quality of one of Queen Koreto's dresses.

# The Principality of Trinidad
## 1893–5

Population: 0
Cause of death: telephones
Today: part of Brazil
///BERET.PRIVATE.DISTORTING

There is the nice Trinidad which everyone knows about, the one in the Caribbean with the beaches and the palm trees, but there is also a comparatively rubbish Trinidad—an island in the Atlantic off the coast of Brazil, full of jagged rocks, the occasional turtle and a lot of miserable crabs.

The PRINCIPALITY of TRINIDAD

SOUTH AMERICA

SOUTH ATLANTIC OCEAN

It was the less-good Trinidad that got the attention of James Harden-Hickey. Born in San Francisco but having moved to republican Paris when he was kid, Harden-Hickey was a fan of royalty in that full-set-of-mail-order-commemorative-Diana-plates kind of way. He started a newspaper that was so offensively pro-monarchy that it led him to multiple duels and dozens of lawsuits. By 1880 he had published 11 novels (some with plots "borrowed" from Jules Verne), most of which were deeply anti-democratic in tone. He also wrote a book about the aesthetics of suicide, which included a list of poisons.

While on his extremely circuitous way to Tibet—having been kicked out of France on account of all the lawsuits—Harden-Hickey noticed a tiny island. It was, so far as he could tell, unclaimed by anyone. Too good an opportunity for a man who despised democracy to ignore, he proclaimed himself James I, Prince of Trinidad.

This "principality" already had a bit of history to it. The Portuguese had tried to settle there years before but gave it up as a bad job. A persistent rumour of buried treasure had seen several expeditions to the island,[30] none of which came to anything. But Harden-Hickey was determined to put the place on the map. Partially bankrolled by his industrialist father-in-law, who he complained about constantly—which seems a little unfair given how much the man seemed to tolerate his son-in-law's stupid schemes—he established an embassy in New York and had a flashy crown designed by a firm of jewellers.

---

[30] Probably lies: the treasure rumour is so stuffed with pirate clichés (dying breath of an old seafarer, etc., etc.), it's amazing anyone ever took it seriously enough to go looking for it. But they did, with one expedition reporting: "[I surveyed] great trenches, the piled-up mounds of earth, the uprooted rocks, with broken wheelbarrows and blocks, worn-out tools, and other relics of our three months strewn over the ground; and it was sad to think that all the energy of these men had been spent in vain.'

He tried to raise some extra cash by establishing an order of chivalry, selling bonds for 200 dollars that would get you free passage to the new kingdom.

Unfortunately for his grand scheme, by 1895 telecommunications had started to be a thing, and the British were laying a transatlantic cable to Brazil. Trinidad happened to be a convenient stopping-off point along the route, and so the British Empire claimed it as their own.[31] The suddenly deposed prince wrote angry letters from his New York embassy denouncing this bit of imperialism.[32] But Harden-Hickey's overly generous father-in-law drew the line at helping him fund a ludicrous plan to get revenge by invading England from Ireland, and so he slipped into a bitter depression. By 1898, widely mocked in the media, he booked into a hotel in El Paso, where he killed himself using one of the poisons suggested in his own book. The *Los Angeles Herald* from the time bleakly noted that "Baron Harden Hickey Prefers to Be a Deceased Gentleman."

---

[31] The British claim to the island, based on the tenuous fact that English astronomer Edmond Halley had once visited it, also failed, and Brazil successfully took it over in 1897. Today it is a Brazilian naval base.

[32] Hickey's New York embassy is now a fashion store.

# The Fiume Endeavour
## 1919–20

POPULATION: 60,000
LANGUAGES: ITALIAN, HUNGARIAN, GERMAN, VENETIAN
CAUSE OF DEATH: TAILS
TODAY: PART OF CROATIA
///TEASPOONS.ROOFTOP.MATTRESS

In the aftermath of World War I, the Big Four powers redrew the map of Europe with the (100 per cent successful) aim of preventing any more trouble in the Balkans. The largely Italian-speaking Fiume ended up in newly formed Yugoslavia. US president Woodrow Wilson earmarked it as a potential HQ for the League of Nations, but the Italian poet Gabriele D'Annunzio—flagrant self-publicist, would-be necromancer, womaniser, terrible teeth—had other ideas.

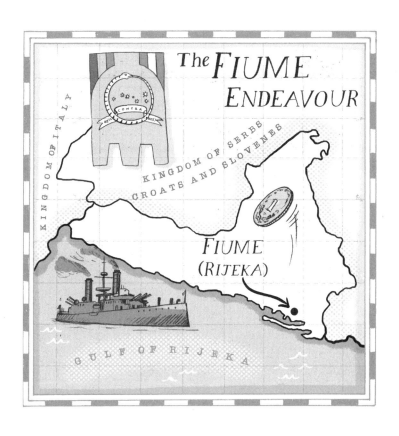

# The *FIUME* ENDEAVOUR

KINGDOM OF ITALY

KINGDOM OF SERBS CROATS AND SLOVENES

FIUME (RIJEKA)

GULF OF RIJEKA

"The eyebrows drawn in such a pure line as to give something indefinably virginal to the melancholy of the big eyes. The beautiful half-open mouth." This is Gabriele D'Annunzio's description of *his own face*. Ernest Hemingway also described him, but typically he was pithier: he thought D'Annunzio was "a jerk."

Evidence to back up Hemingway's opinion:

- D'Annunzio's kids weren't allowed to call him "papa," they had to call him "maestro."
- He got out of a lunch date by sending his chauffeur to explain that "he's gone up in a balloon and might not be back for ages."
- He basically invented all the trappings of fascism that still hang about today.

In September 1919, D'Annunzio drove into the city of Fiume at the head of his "legionnaires," an ultra-violent piratical fan rabble. The Italian army—expressly ordered to stop him—gave a collective "more than my pay grade" shrug and let him continue on his way. As an ardent nationalist, D'Annunzio's intention was to claim Fiume on behalf of Italy, but Italy—or at least the government of Prime Minister Francesco Nitti—didn't want anything to do with this circus. So, having taken the place over, he found himself in charge of his own tiny fiefdom, and set about making it a "beacon for the world." This translated as "a lot of ice cream and borderline anarchy."

Beyond really liking torpedoes and thinking that death was sexy, D'Annunzio couldn't be said to have a coherent political philosophy, but he very much enjoyed styling it out. He issued decrees and proclamations and nailed them up around town, only to change his mind and issue a contradictory set later the same day. He decked everywhere out with flowers, because he was a big fan of flowers. If you could ignore the occasional lynching and didn't mind the endless speeches crammed with those rhetorical flourishes that dictators everywhere would soon adopt as their own, life in Fiume was a party. D'Annunzio even appointed World War I flying ace Guido Keller as his "Action Secretary." Keller, a keen naturist, spent as much time as possible naked, and slept in the same bed as his pet eagle. It is also said that he once crashed his plane in a field next to a donkey, took a shine to the donkey while doing repairs, strapped the donkey to his plane's fuselage and flew it back to Fiume as a gift for his boss.

Things got serious when, after putting up with more than a year of this kind of roguery, an Italian warship parked in the bay shelled D'Annunzio's palace. He had a decision to make. Showing all the profound, grown-up sense of responsibility he was famous for, he flipped a coin: it came up tails, and so he called it a day. His Fiume Endeavour ("Impresa di Fiume") died on a coin toss.

While the newly rechristened Free State of Fiume carried on for another three years without him,[33] D'Annunzio retired to his spectacularly creepy house overlooking Lake Garda, where he was showered with gifts by Mussolini in order to keep him out of trouble (Mussolini was operating on the principle that "either you pull the tooth, or you fill it with gold.") In 1938 he died of a brain haemorrhage at his desk. Or possibly he was poisoned by his girlfriend, a Nazi spy planted to keep tabs on him—as with most of D'Annunzio's life, the truth is murky.[34]

---

[33] After D'Annunzio, Fiume didn't get a lot of rest: first carved up by Italy and Yugoslavia, then occupied by the Germans, then finding itself back in Yugoslavia, and currently part of Croatia (in Croatian it is called Rijeka).

[34] Probably lies: D'Annunzio enjoyed spreading a lot of myths about himself. He'd have dinner parties and comment that children tasted like lamb, but he almost certainly didn't eat children.

# THE KINGDOM OF SEDANG
## 1888–90

POPULATION: UNKNOWN
CAPITAL: KON TUM
LANGUAGES: SEDANG, FRENCH
CAUSE OF DEATH: A KING WHO WAS TOO SHADY BY HALF
TODAY: PART OF VIETNAM
///WISTFULNESS.TOOTHBRUSH.BIDDING

There's a strangely consistent psychological profile that fits Guys Who Set Up Countries. Dead dad, raised by a doting mum, serially unfaithful, stint in the army or navy, writer or journalist, can't be trusted with money, fantasist—these could all more or less describe D'Annunzio in Fiume, or Harden-Hickey in Trinidad, or Theodore von Neuhoff in Corsica, or Exhibit D: Marie-Charles David de Mayréna.

Growing up in France, where he was awarded the Legion of Honour for bravery during the Franco-Prussian War, in 1883 de Mayréna was accused of "swindling." He fled to Holland, and then to the Dutch East Indies, from which he was forcibly repatriated. Undeterred, he was soon heading out east again, having somehow been entrusted with 30,000 francs to lead an expedition to unexplored Java, even though he was the last person anyone should have been entrusting 30,000 francs to. He only made it as far as Saigon, where he lived it up in cafés, told tall tales and spent all the expedition money. The local police kept a file on him.

Over the next few years, he undertook a number of forays into the interior of Indochina, supposedly to negotiate with the natives on behalf of the French. In 1888, he landed on the coast of Quinton, in modern-day Vietnam. There the indigenous tribes practised a basic form of agriculture and lived in villages built around *rongs*, houses on stilts with huge, pointed thatched roofs. In one of these, de Mayréna signed a treaty with a collection of the local chiefs, unifying the disparate groups into a confederation—but rather than a confederation proclaiming loyalty to France, it was one that proclaimed loyalty to Marie the First, King of Sedang. Exactly how and why this happened is unclear, but some put it down to "his skill at prestidigitation" (i.e., he was good at doing magic tricks). He came up with a national anthem (based on can-can music) and declared Catholicism the state religion, though he himself adopted Islam because it allowed him to take multiple wives.

King Marie travelled to Hong Kong to swank about and raise more funds. Initially, the local press lapped him up, impressed by his charm and very swish outfits. But rumours soon started to circulate. Local tailors dogged him for payment of outstanding bills for his cartoonish uniforms. His reputation suffering, he headed back to Paris where—another common theme, this—he tried to bestow honours in exchange for cash.

At various points he tried to sell his entire kingdom to France,[35] Prussia and the British, but none of them were interested. Finally, he found a credulous sap: a rich Belgian industrialist who was obsessed with titles, which Marie was happy to shower him with. This funded his return to Indochina, but when he stopped off in Singapore he learned that the French now claimed Sedang and the surrounding region as their own, and had blockaded the port. Fearing they would try to extradite him (both on account of the earlier "swindling" and the questionable, self-aggrandising way in which he had performed his "negotiations") he headed for home. But he never quite got that far, instead finishing up on the island of Tioman, in the South China Sea. And that's where he spent the rest of his life, in a shack with a man who made a living collecting bird nests, becoming increasingly paranoid about threats to his life—until one day, when out taking his French poodle, Auguste,[36] for a walk, he was bitten by a deadly snake.[37]

[35] To be exact, he tried to blackmail France into buying Sedang by threatening to otherwise sell it to the Brits, which did little to help his popularity with either of them.

[36] " . . . the natives of the place will point out to you a number of strange-looking quadrupeds, half-pariah, half-poodle, and with pride will inform you that these are French Dogs; and these uncouth descendants of the well-beloved and redoubtable Auguste are the only traces left upon this little fairy island marking it as the erstwhile refuge of Marie David de Mayrena, King of the Sedangs."—Sir Hugh Clifford, *Heroes of Exile* (1906)

[37] Conflicting reports at the time suggest that Marie's death might alternatively have been the result of either a duel or poisoning, so it's possible he wasn't as paranoid as he seemed.

# Mistakes & Micronations

# THE REPUBLIC OF COSPAIA
## 1440–1826

POPULATION: CIRCA 300
LANGUAGE: ITALIAN
CAUSE OF DEATH: TOO MUCH OF A GOOD THING
TODAY: PART OF ITALY
///FIRMER.IMPERIALISM.DELAYS

Things were going badly for Pope Eugene IV. Years of ugly church politics, accusations of corruption and favouritism, competing claims about who even counted as the real pope in the first place—it had all led to a lot of senior Catholics adopting Father Ted's favourite get-out line when presented with a difficult question: "*That would be an ecumenical matter.*" By which they meant that the buck should stop not with the pope, but with an ecumenical council of "experts." Eugene, who enjoyed being the undisputed word of God, felt differently.

Bitter ecclesiastical power struggles are expensive, and Eugene needed funds, so he did what anyone would do when they're skint: he went to the fifteenth-century equivalent of a pawn shop, the Medici family, and put down a chunk of papal territory as collateral for 25,000 gold florins. Armed with this war chest, Eugene eventually got his way, but—unable to repay the loan—he signed over the promised real estate to his creditors. And then the man who had just won an argument about how extremely infallible he was screwed up. They agreed to a border on a river. Neither side seemed to notice that the river was one of two tributaries, and so each drew their respective border at the nearest bank—of different bits of river. This left a small chunk of land, occupied by the hitherto unremarkable village of Cospaia, stranded in the middle, unclaimed by anyone. Not for the last time, a nation was formed by cartographical accident.

Cospaians were quick to pick up on the salient point of this: free from taxes and papal law, they proclaimed themselves an independent republic. They set about the fun part—designing a flag and coat of arms—but didn't get as far as dealing with the duller business of electing a government. Instead, they continued with the vague, unofficial "council of elders" common to most isolated Italian villages back then.

A hundred years later, still ignored by everyone, Cospaia properly hit its stride with the arrival of tobacco in Europe.[38] The Catholic Church didn't approve, because not approving of things was kind of its whole deal, and threatened to excommunicate anybody who produced the stuff. Cospaia, outside of papal jurisdiction and with the perfect climate for growing the

---

[38] Initially thought to have medicinal properties when first imported into Europe, it was, in 1563, a Swiss doctor who noted that "the tobacco leaf also has a wonderful power of producing a kind of peaceful drunkeness."

tobacco plant, suddenly found itself with a near-monopoly in the region. It was the start of a 250-year-long boom time.

Throughout history, the unwritten rule of micronations is that you keep your head down, stay off the radar and hope that the bigger kids will leave you alone. But Cospaia's thriving free-for-all started to niggle. By the nineteenth century it had supposedly become "a haven for draft dodgers and other undesirables." Then Pope Leo XI and the neighbouring Grand Duke Leopold II started up territorial negotiations again. The Cospaians, wise to their own predicament, didn't attempt to go out in a blaze of glory but instead opted for a blaze of cigarettes: they agreed to be reabsorbed, but with a special dispensation to keep growing their tobacco.

The unforeseen legacy of the Pope's mistake is that now, 500 years later, irritating teen anarchist-types clog up the internet telling people that "actually anarchy is really good, look at the Republic of Cospaia, they survived for 400 years without a government so I don't see why I should clean my room."

# NEW CALEDONIA
## 1698–1700

POPULATION: 1,200 (BUT NOT FOR LONG)
CAPITAL: NEW EDINBURGH
CURRENCY: COMBS
CAUSE OF DEATH: BAD PLANNING, MOSQUITOES, SASSENACHS
TODAY: PART OF PANAMA
///DOVES.UNSTAINED.MUSICIANS

It's comforting to feel smug about the past. We laugh at our disasters and our haircuts and our computers the size of a bus. "Look at those olden-days idiots! How could they be so incredibly lame? Not like me, living in the glorious now, knowing all the things I know. This housing market is never going to crash!" With the benefit of hindsight, Scotland's attempt to establish New Caledonia seems so obviously doomed it's risible—but the scheme wasn't quite the straight-up bit of stupidity it's usually portrayed as.

As usual, the English were definitely partly to blame. Scotland's economy was in a bad way, and one of the reasons was that England, and the ever-rapacious East India Company, refused to allow it any bite of the international trading pie. The Company of Scotland was an attempt to fight back. It planned to raise funds in order to kick-start a new Scottish empire. That in itself wasn't a bad idea. But the next issue was "where," and this is the point things started to unravel.

Bad luck would have it that Lionel Wafer, a Welsh explorer, had returned from what is now Panama some years previously and made it sound amazing: green jungle, clear streams, delicious wild hogs, giant rabbits, fat bees, grassy meadows, prickly pears and pineapples as big as your head. For people stuck in rainy, impoverished Edinburgh, it sounded like a literal paradise. The Company decided it had found the perfect place to set up its trading colony, and the Darien scheme was born. Nobody stopped to ask why, if this Darien place was as great as all that, the Spanish hadn't already taken it over the way they had the rest of the Americas.

The plan instantly hit a snag when England banned the Company of Scotland from seeking investors in either London or the Netherlands. So, it had to turn to its countrymen: thousands of small investors who enthusiastically backed the project to the tune of 400,000 pounds, which was a *staggering* amount, equivalent to an entire fifth of the country's economy. Boats were purchased and colonists were recruited—and it seemed, for a moment, that the English wouldn't have it all their own way for once.

The stuff they packed appears absurd now but would have struck your average seventeenth-century Scot as essential. Combs to exchange with the indigenous tribes, loads of Bibles, bonnets galore and a massive amount of whiskey. In 1698, five ships set out, carrying a total of 1,200 people. The journey was difficult, and things got worse when they arrived. The locals weren't that interested in the combs. The settlers couldn't locate a source of fresh water. The swampy location they'd chosen wasn't much like Wafer's description, and several billion mosquitoes meant malaria was rife. The death rate ran at about ten a day. The only upside was that it was 300 years too early for Bear Grylls to show up.

The sailors, refusing to leave their boats, didn't trust the colonists and vice versa. The local Kuna people proved friendly enough—like the Scots, they hated the Spanish—but there was a limit as to what they could do to help. Everybody got very drunk—though given the prevalence of waterborne diseases, sticking to booze wasn't the dumbest strategy in the world.

After only a year, with the population down to 300, the colonists abandoned New Edinburgh and sailed for New York. Unfortunately, news was slow in 1699, and an initial flurry of positive letters sent out as a PR campaign—suspiciously, in retrospect, featuring the recurring phrase "one of the fruitfullest spots of ground on the face of the Earth!"—had already led to a second batch of settlers striking out for the new country. Upon arrival, one of their boats caught fire. The colony was besieged by the Spanish. The Scots abandoned it once again in 1700.[39] Back home the Company collapsed in ignominy. As a result, New Caledonia wasn't the only nation to officially come unstuck—Scotland would, before the decade was out, find itself having to sign the Acts of Union, tying itself to England for at least another three hundred and twenty years, in part because the Darien scheme had left it bankrupt.

---

[39] The Company of Scotland tried to recoup its losses after that by launching two more ships, the crews of which promptly palled about with some pirates, then did a deal to lend the pirates their boats, then backed out of the deal, then had their boats nicked by the pirates anyway.

Today you can drive 19,000 miles along the Pan-American Highway all the way from Alaska to the tip of Argentina . . . except for the Darién Gap, still too much of a swampy challenge even for the smart, nowadays version of us.

## THE PRINCIPALITY OF ELBA
### 1814–15

POPULATION: 12,000
CAPITAL: PORTOFERRAIO
LANGUAGES: ITALIAN, FRENCH
CURRENCY: FRANCS
CAUSE OF DEATH: BOREDOM
TODAY: PART OF ITALY
///COOKIES.SWAN.JUDGES

It had been a rough few years and, like desperate parents sticking an iPad in front of their difficult toddler, the great powers of Europe decided to give the recently vanquished Emperor Napoleon a little country of his own to play with. "It'll keep him out of trouble," went the slightly flawed reasoning. "He'll grow some pumpkins and settle down and it'll all be fine. He probably just had too much sugar."

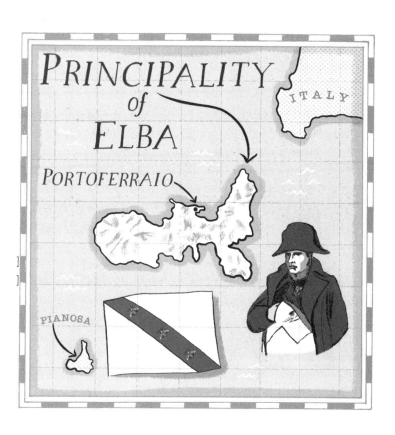

So began the short-lived life of Elba as a sovereign nation. Measuring 18 miles from tip-to-tip, it was 1/4,000 the size of Napoleon's previous place. The underwhelming capital, Portoferraio, lacked the glamour of nineteenth-century Paris, but when Napoleon stepped off his boat, he did his best to look impressed at the bountiful natural resources of "some cabbages" and "some dust." In a welcoming ceremony, the local mayor gave him the keys to the town—though in fact they were the mayor's cellar keys, painted gold, because the actual ceremonial keys had gotten lost. This pretty much set the tone.[40]

Instead of having a sulk about what a comedown it all was, Napoleon, to his credit, threw himself into making the place less terrible. He started a drive to grow more potatoes and radishes, and built anti-pirate fortifications. He erected schools and laid proper streets and even announced that, from now on, "no more than five people should have to share a bed."

Despite this initial enthusiasm, it turned out that putting up new lampposts and digging in his garden weren't as stimulating as invading Russia.[41] Napoleon fell into a funk. He ate a lot of biscuits. He played cards with his mum. A steady stream of spies dropped by to keep tabs on him and he pretended not to notice them. Meanwhile, back in Paris, the government planted a load of scandalous stories in the press about how the former emperor was not only riddled with various diseases but was also sleeping with his own sister. The smear campaign was sup-

[40] Probably lies: Napoleon's first words upon arriving on the island were not "Able was I ere I saw Elba"—he did not speak in confusing English palindromes.

[41] In a sign that he was possibly not a completely reformed character, Napoleon instantly annexed the nearby island of Pianosa, where he planned to grow wheat.

posed to turn the public against him. It didn't work—all it did was make Napoleon feel more aggrieved. Who were these moral pygmies to disrespect a man of his giant (if entirely metaphorical) stature?

So, he painted a boat with the English colours, had a final dinner with his mum and sister, and escaped back to France, where he started up his oversized game of Risk again. After Waterloo, where he came unstuck for the second time, the European powers learned their lesson and put his new naughty step in the middle of the Atlantic, on the bleak windswept speck that was St. Helena, which they made very clear he wasn't a king of. This is where Napoleon would see out his days—thinking wistfully about how maybe Elba wasn't that bad after all—until his death, which was possibly caused by arsenic in his wallpaper.[42]

[42] Becoming part of the newly unified Italy in 1860, today Elba has a flourishing population of mouflon, a type of horned sheep introduced in the 1970s, which some locals now want to cull because they mess up the olive groves.

# FRANCEVILLE
## 1889–90

POPULATION: 540
LANGUAGES: LOTS
CURRENCY: PIGS
CAUSE OF DEATH: BORN A HUNDRED YEARS TOO EARLY
TODAY: PART OF VANUATU
///TIPPING.SCARY.BLURTS

In terms of "natural disasters," Vanuatu is rated by the UN as the number-one riskiest place in the world—beating out Tonga, Guatemala and Bangladesh.[43] By the seventeenth century a constant barrage of earthquakes and hurricanes had led the indigenous Ni-Vanuatu people to develop a "patient tolerance for calamity."[44] Which was lucky, because the Europeans were about to turn up, and that always goes well.

[43] As if life there wasn't already fragile enough, it was the inhabitants of Vanuatu who invented bungee jumping, using vines and rickety towers.
[44] Noted in the Pacific Island Discussion Papers, 1999, World Bank.

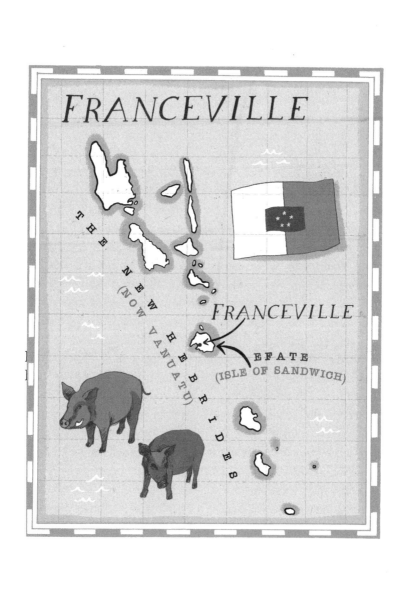

FRANCEVILLE

THE NEW HEBRIDES (NOW VANUATU)

FRANCEVILLE

EFATE
(ISLE OF SANDWICH)

The archipelago of Vanuatu is made up of about 80 islands. It has a bountiful supply of coconuts and a possibly over-bountiful supply of languages: 113. That averages out as one language per 15,000 people. The most important currency was—and to an extent, still is—pigs.[45]

Initially settled by the Melanesians, the seventeenth century brought the arrival of the Portuguese and their usual crappy gifts of whooping cough and influenza. The first visitor was the explorer Pedro Fernandes de Queirós, who, in the grand tradition of explorers getting everything wrong, mistakenly believed he had discovered the rumoured Great Southern Continent. It would be 160 years until the next European encounter, when French explorer Louis-Antoine de Bougainville paid a cursory visit. A few years later Captain Cook sailed through, cheerily christening the islands "the New Hebrides." Cook was followed by assorted whalers and would-be sandalwood traders. They found the locals difficult to deal with. When the *British Sovereign* sank in 1847, the surviving crew swam ashore only to be killed and eaten. Relations were not off to a great start.

But the traders and newly arrived missionaries persisted. They set up plantations and exchanged goods for land, though the Ni-Vanuatu had no concept of land ownership. Then more unlucky missionaries turned up and got eaten. Just as the British were starting to think this was all maybe more trouble than it was worth, the French arrived. Supremely petty in the way that superpowers tend to be, the Brits instantly decided that they were damned if they were going to let their old enemy take control of the islands, cannibals or no.

Colonialism gets a deservedly bad rap, but there is something almost as bad: half-arsed, sort-of-but-not-quite colonialism. This was the fate of the New Hebrides, caught between two imperial

---

[45] The most valuable and sought-after type of pig in Vanuatu is the "hairless hermaphrodite pig" from the island of Malo.

dads spoiling for a fight. To stop the rivalry devolving into a full-blown war, Britain and France reached an agreement: the archipelago would be under the guard of a joint naval commission. What this actually meant was general lawlessness and no proper government.

Some neglected "in between" nations like the Republic of Cospaia (*see* page 76) run with this state of affairs and never look back. But the inhabitants—both native and colonist—of the New Hebrides didn't find it particularly appealing, and pious missionaries were especially fed up that they couldn't legally get married. So, in Franceville (now Port Vila) on the island of Efate, they decided to do something about it.

They announced themselves as an independent commune, hoping to establish some basis in international law. They unveiled a flag and appointed a president. A constitution was drawn up. This tiny enclave became one of the very first nations to practise universal suffrage, regardless of race, gender or creed. Though obviously you could only get elected if you were a white male, let's not get carried away, guys.

Then, like an unappealing couple in a geopolitical romcom, the British and the French suddenly managed to see past their rivalry and realised they had loads in common: namely that they were both greedy old reactionaries who weren't going to let people think self-governing was an option, because that was the kind of talk that brought down empires. So, they sent their boats in to dismantle Franceville. A problem had been dealt with, but the untreated cause of that problem went on to fester. And a hundred years later it would erupt again, in the unlikely form of a messianic bulldozer driver and the "Republic of Vemerana" . . .

# The Republic of Vemerana
## May–September 1980

POPULATION: 40,000
CURRENCY: PIGS
CAUSE OF DEATH: A COCONUT WAR
TODAY: PART OF VANUATU
///TARDY.SCRAP.INTENSIFIED

The Phoenix Foundation sounds like something from the hackier end of the Bond movies, one of those shadowy cabals of evil, big-business types who have meetings in a hollowed-out volcano. Which isn't too far off the mark. Michael Oliver was a real-estate millionaire from Nevada. Harry D. Schultz published a popular newsletter about how to avoid taxes (Margaret Thatcher being an avid subscriber). Both were fed up at having to pay for boring things like roads and hospitals that they might not personally use, and about having to obey laws that might not personally suit them, so they came up with a predictable rich-guy plan: start a new, totally libertarian country.

They'd already tried with the Republic of Minerva, a half-submerged reef in Tonga, but that hadn't panned out because it was a deeply stupid idea. An effort to get a tax haven going in the Bahamas also came to nothing. Third time's the charm, so they tried again in 1980, now targeting the island of Espiritu Santo.[46] It was here they got involved with bearded, messianic, half-Scottish former bulldozer driver Jimmy Stevens, who also went by the name "Moses." He was already head of the New Hebrides Autonomy Movement, which—a little counter-intuitively perhaps—was campaigning *against* the imminent autonomy of the New Hebrides (on the cusp of becoming the nation of Vanuatu).[47] Jimmy Stevens called, in a slightly vague, cultish way, for a return to "the old ways:" a respect for the local beliefs and social structure that had been messed up by years of neglectful French-British joint rule. He issued a set of badges showing various ranks in the movement, from his own badge—"chief president"—all the way down to the slightly less important rank of "school children's guard." Funded to the tune of $ 250,000 by the Phoenix Foundation (and bliss-fully unaware that his personal aims only represented Phase One of their sinister plan), Stevens led an uprising on the island, blockaded the airport, blew up a couple of bridges and proclaimed the Republic of Vemerana.

The New Hebrides government tried to get the British to help out, but the French hadn't shaken that old sense of rivalry and forbade it. So, it was down to nearby Papua New Guinea to send a small force, starting what the foreign press patronis-ingly dubbed the "Coconut War." It wasn't much of a conflict. Stevens's followers were armed with bows and arrows, and the

---

[46] A cult on one of the islands today worships Prince Philip, which sug-gests a shortage of decent stuff to worship.

[47] There were two political parties, and both wanted slightly different types of self-determination. Stevens's version placed a lot more emphasis on free love/multiple wives.

islanders were mostly quite friendly to the Papua New Guineans. When his son was shot after driving through a road-block, a distraught Stevens declared that he had never meant for anyone to get hurt and the movement quickly fell apart. The Pacific Moses surrendered and wound up sentenced to 14 years in prison.[48] The New Hebrides became Vanuatu. Somewhere, the Phoenix Foundation no doubt continues to do its slightly shadowy thing.

[48] Jimmy was let out of prison four years early, on the condition that he paid the government the sum of 30 pigs.

A long with a nice flag and a hummable anthem, an important attribute for any new country is a catchy name. Ideally, something succinct like "Spain" or "Chad." At a stretch you could go with a bit more of a mouthful like "The United States of America" or "Papua New Guinea." Or, if you really want to push the boat out, why not try:

THE SOVIET REPUBLIC OF SOLDIERS
& FORTRESS-BUILDERS OF NAISSAAR
DECEMBER 1917–FEBRUARY 1918

POPULATION: <500
CAUSE OF DEATH: GERMANY
TODAY: PART OF ESTONIA
///FORESIGHT.GROW.DAZZLE

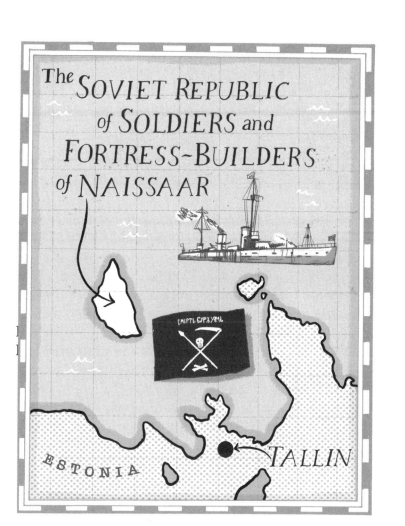

The SOVIET REPUBLIC of SOLDIERS and FORTRESS-BUILDERS of NAISSAAR

СМЕРТЬ БУРЖУЯМ

TALLIN

ESTONIA

The USSR had an untidy start. It doesn't matter how neat your beards or slogans are, you can't take over something the size of the Russian Empire in a day. When the Bolsheviks' October Revolution rippled out from St. Petersburg, it did so in fits and spurts. General confusion ensued. An improbable number of self-declared nation states popped up in a matter of months: the Republic of North Ingria, the Duchy of Courland and Semigallia, the Hutsul Republic, the Lemko Republic, the Crimean People's Republic, the Kuban People's Republic, the Kars Republic, the Don Republic, the North Caucasian Emirate, the Trans-Caucasian Federation, the Republic of Idel-Ural, the Alash Autonomy, Kokand, Basmachi, Green Ukraine. *This isn't even a complete list.* If you haven't heard of them, it's because for the most part they fizzled out virtually before they'd even got going.

One of these damselflies was the Soviet Republic of Soldiers and Fortress-Builders. In the Gulf of Finland, in the icy seas between Tallinn and Helsinki, lies the pine-covered island of Naissaar. The name translates as "Island of Women," which has led some to suggest it might be the same Island of Women, home to a mythical race of Amazons, recorded by Adam of Bremen a thousand years ago. But by 1917 it was populated by dour fishermen and the inhabitants of a recently constructed Russian fortress. In the muddle of revolutionary fervour sweeping through the continent, the crew of a nearby battle-ship, the *Petropavlovsk*—under the command of charismatic anarcho-syndicalist[49] Stepan Petrichenko—decided to seize the island. The 80-strong crew appointed commissars of finance, health and education. They also supposedly levied taxes on the locals, though this doesn't sound particularly anarcho-syndicalist of them.

---

[49] The simplest definition of anarcho-syndicalism is probably "the system medieval peasant Michael Palin subscribes to in *Monty Python and the Holy Grail.*"

The newly independent Estonian government didn't take kindly to what they viewed as opportunistic piracy rather than legitimate nation building, but because Estonia was promptly invaded by the German Empire, they didn't have a chance to do much about it. It was the Germans who drove the revolutionaries off the island, barely two months after they'd arrived. The *Petropavlovsk* sailed off to Kronstadt, where Petrichenko and his crew started the rebellion that came as close as anybody to toppling the increasingly dictatorial Bolsheviks.[50] The republic of fortress builders was forgotten, and is now a nature reserve, littered with the old naval mines that were manufactured there.

[50] After Trotsky crushed the Kronstadt uprising, Petrichenko fled to Finland, but was later deported back to the USSR. He died in Russia's largest jail.

# NEUTRAL MORESNET
## 1816–1920

POPULATION: 3,000
CAPITAL: KELMIS
LANGUAGES: DUTCH, FRENCH, GERMAN, ESPERANTO
CAUSE OF DEATH: ZINC DEFICIENCY
TODAY: PART OF BELGIUM
///TODDLER.PASSIONS.BLOCKING

After Napoleon smashed Europe to pieces, the Congress of Vienna was a grand attempt to glue everything back together. It aimed to create a more stable balance of power, especially between distrustful neighbours Prussia and the Netherlands. These two rivals tried to thrash out a deal and draw a map everyone liked, but they found themselves with a sticking point. A mountain. More specifically: the mountain's zinc mine.

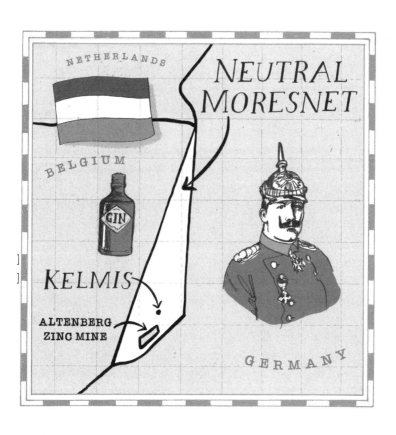

Nineteenth-century Europe was about to get heavily into the steampunk aesthetic, and for that you needed zinc, which outside of Bristol was in short supply. Neither country wanted to let the other get their hands on such a valuable resource. The solution: they decided it would belong to nobody. An awkward triangle of "neutral" territory was created, and the fact that this meant the people living there would be technically stateless didn't seem to bother any of those in charge. Suddenly free from conscription, the war-weary inhabitants didn't mind their disenfranchisement too much either.

The company that owned the mine controlled everything: it was the main employer, it ran the bank, the shops and the hospital. Which was fine, until inevitably, in 1885, the zinc ran out. Neutral Moresnet, having displayed a distinct lack of foresight, found itself in dire need of an economy. They set up a casino, because casinos had been banned in their new neighbour, Belgium.[51] But pointy-hatted killjoy Kaiser Wilhelm II didn't approve and threatened to annex them, so the casino shut down. A different Wilhelm—the keen philatelist and local physician Dr. Wilhelm Molly—had a go at issuing stamps, hoping that stamp collectors would provide a much-needed revenue stream.[52] But that was thwarted by the Belgians. More successful were the gin distilleries. Bars and cafés also flourished—there were upwards of 70, which is quite a lot for a place that started off with 50 houses and a church.

Moresnet developed a boozy, semi-lawless reputation (there was one single policeman, who spent most of his time in a café playing chess), which the mayor tried to curb by announcing

---

[51] Belgium had gained independence from the Netherlands in 1830 and was about to engage in its own bit of hyper-horrific country creation (*see* page 202).

[52] One stamp collector got so fed up with a French magazine stealing his articles about stamps, he made up an entirely fake Neutral Moresnet stamp and wrote about it to troll them.

that "the singing of dirty songs is to be prohibited." Then, in 1908, Dr. Molly had another idea he hoped would be a money-spinner: Neutral Moresnet would become the first and only Esperanto-speaking state. The populace threw a party, wrote a national anthem, and the country's new name was unveiled—Amikejo, which means "place of friendship" in Esperanto.

As business plans go, it's not clear how becoming a nation of Esperanto speakers was going to make their fortune. And the kaiser, demonstrating almost no *amikejo* at all, continued to find the country irritating, repeatedly cutting off its electricity supply. Finally, World War I hove into view and Amikejo was *fuŝado* (screwed).

In the aftermath, at yet another post-war conference, the now strategically insignificant triangle of land was unceremoniously awarded to Belgium. But the Esperanto society still holds an annual *disko* (disco) there, which is *bona* (nice).[53]

---

[53] Useful phrases in Esperanto according to Google Translate: The entire concept of the nation state is complicated. *La tuta koncepto de la nacioŝtato estas komplika.* Would you like to buy some gin? *Ĉu vi ŝatus aĉeti gin?* This Kaiser guy seems like a bastard. *Ĉi tiu Kaiser-ulo ŝajnas kiel bastardo.*

# The Republic of Perloja
## 1918–23

POPULATION: CIRCA 700
LANGUAGE: DZUKIAN (LITHUANIAN DIALECT)
CURRENCY: "PERLOJA LITAS"
CAUSE OF DEATH: NEW MAPS
TODAY: PART OF LITHUANIA
///UNHAPPY.SEIZURE.TWEETERS

They even had one spy. He was lame, but he could imitate the voices of birds and animals; he could change his clothes to look like an old woman."—Anne Applebaum, *Between East and West*

Grand Duke Vytautas was the greatest figure in Lithuanian history—along with his very talented horse, who according to myth once got rid of a flood simply by drinking it. Vytautas built his first church in the village of Perloja on Lithuania's southern border, and then in 1387, having taken a shine to the place, he supposedly granted it a special charter, decreeing that no inhabitant could ever become a serf. When—many years later—a grasping landlord decided that he actually quite fancied having a few local serfs, Vytautas proved good to his word: Lithuanian soldiers turned up and dealt with the landlord in the way that everyone would like to deal with landlords.

But by 1918, World War I was grinding to an end, Europe was a wreck, and everything was up for grabs. The Russian Empire had collapsed to the Bolsheviks, the Germans were sweeping through the region—even though they knew they'd lost—and a resurgent Poland was trying to get whatever territory it could come by. Borders were being redrawn everywhere and the Perlojans were worried their long links with Vytautas and his magic horse would be lost in the reshuffle. They sent an envoy to meet the League of Nations representative at Vilnius. It didn't go well; the problems of a tiny East European village didn't figure highly on the League's to-do list. It waved them away.

Back in Perloja they held a meeting in their little square, next to the statue of Vytautas, and discussed the problem. One thing led to another, speeches were given, people got emotional, and by the end of the day they had proclaimed themselves a republic. They already had a coat of arms that they could use as a flag (a bison with a cross on his head, so pretty good as far as national emblems go). They elected a prime minister, a minister of the interior, a finance minister and a judge. The judge was popular for his wise sentencing of a wife-beater to be beaten by his wife. A drunken priest was put in charge of the army—300 local men with home-made uniforms. Plans were drawn up for a local currency with Vytautas on it. And, of course, they had their lone spy who could do bird impressions and dress as an old woman.[54]

As they had feared, the redrawn map put most of the village on the Polish side of the border. The Polish police would turn up, and the Perlojans would hide in caves until they'd gone. A number of skirmishes culminated in the villagers attacking what they thought were Polish border guards but who turned out to be a Lithuanian unit—the very people they were trying to remain loyal to. Realising the hopelessness of the fight, they put down their arms and reluctantly agreed to abide by the laws of Poland, though they commemorated their bold independent stand with a plaque. The Soviets would later invade, restoring Perloja to Lithuania but also deporting trucks full of locals to the gulags. Neither they nor the Nazis would manage to pull down the statue of Vytautas, despite their best efforts.

[54] Obviously being able to change your clothes "to look like an old woman" isn't that impressive. In World War I, French soldiers disguised themselves as a (papier-mâché) horse carcass to get close to the German trenches.

# The Quilombo of Palmares
## 1606–94

Population: circa 11,000
Cause of death: outside of Hollywood plucky underdogs don't actually win
Today: part of Brazil
///physics.butter.duck

INT—Hollywood Studio—Day

HIGH-POWERED EXEC: Hit me with the pitch, kid.

HACK WRITER: We open in Brazil. Misty forests, very exotic. A baby—our hero, Zumbi—is stolen from a besieged micronation of escaped African slaves. He's brought up by a kindly priest. There's an exciting training montage, and then, as a teen, he runs away from his adopted home, back to the place of his birth, where he proves to be a brilliant soldier, ultimately leading a bold resistance against an evil, racist empire. Plus, there's a sad bit at the end to keep it Oscarworthy.

HIGH-POWERED EXEC: I like it.

HACK WRITER: Great! I was worried it might be a bit too on the nose.

HIGH-POWERED EXEC: This heroic black slave, do we think Scarlett Johansson might be a good fit?

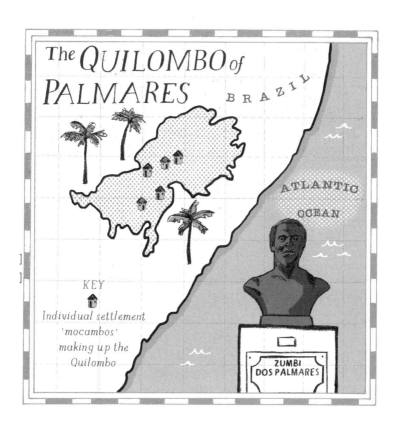

The QUILOMBO of PALMARES

BRAZIL

ATLANTIC
OCEAN

KEY

Individual settlement
'mocambos'
making up the
Quilombo

ZUMBI
DOS PALMARES

By the end of the sixteenth century, Brazil was dominated by two European powers, Portugal and the Netherlands, both big fans of slavery. Many of the slaves tried to escape. A few were successful. A steady trickle of former plantation workers headed for the forested interior, and by around 1606 some of them had established a *quilombo*—a conglomeration of "towns," or *mocambos*, ruled by a single king—near Recife. For all intents and purposes this was a tiny country of its own, a piece of Africa in South America. It was christened "Los Palmares" because of the preponderance of palm trees. A bit like the indomitable Gaulish village in *Asterix*, a wooden palisade surrounded the settlements. Within the palisade ran ditches filled with spikes.

The few descriptions we have are all from people who were trying to attack Palmares. The *quilombo* got battered; between 1654 and 1678 we know of at least 20 Portuguese expeditions against it. In between these raids, the little state would take a breather and trade with its neighbours: food and crafts for salt and weapons. But the plantation owners were keen to be rid of such an obvious beacon for their workforce to escape to.

It was during a Portuguese raid in 1655 that the infant Zumbi was captured and given to Father Melo, a priest living in the coastal town of Porto Calvo. There, Zumbi was raised as the priest's protégé. After he ran away back to Palmares he would sometimes secretly slip out to pay his old mentor visits.

The Portuguese attacks continued unabated. Zumbi fast became the kingdom's best fighter, "skilled with firearms, swords, lances and arrows." In 1678, tired of constant war, the King of Palmares, Ganga Zumba, sought a deal with the Portuguese: a treaty would guarantee his sovereignty, but it required fugitive slaves to be returned to their former owners. The populace was unimpressed. The details are vague, but some sort of regicide went down, and Zumbi was crowned the new king.

Under Zumbi's leadership, the kingdom survived another 15 years. But in a final cinematic flourish, the Portuguese turned to a hired gun: "Bush Captain" Domingos Jorge Velho, a famous "wilderness tamer." His band of brigands besieged Palmares for three weeks. In a climactic battle, 500 Palmarinos were captured and another 500 killed—200 of whom were hurled off a precipice. According to some accounts, Zumbi himself escaped and continued to wage a guerrilla war against the Portuguese until—betrayed by one of his own men—he was finally ambushed and killed. His reputation was such by this point that the Portuguese felt it necessary to display his head on a pike in the local capital, as proof that he wasn't a god.[55]

[55] Today, Zumbi has an international airport named after him. He also gets a mention in a song by the Brazilian heavy metal band Sepultura.

# THE FREE STATE OF BOTTLENECK
## 1919–23

POPULATION: 17,000
CAPITAL: LORCH
LANGUAGE: GERMAN
CAUSE OF DEATH: DEBT COLLECTION BY FRANCE
TODAY: PART OF GERMANY
///NATIONALITY.ENGINEER.SKULLS

Another war, another attempt to redraw the map, another total mess. The "will this do?" back-of-an-envelope approach with which these post-cataclysm conferences went about things is both impressively louche and depressingly familiar.

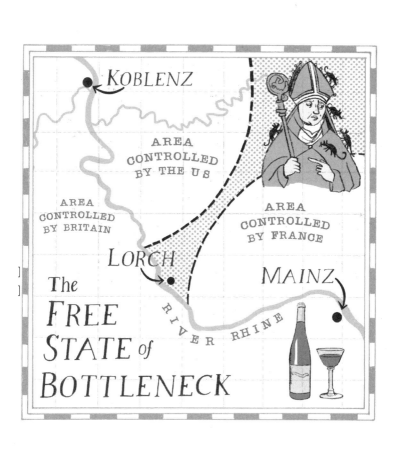

KOBLENZ

AREA
CONTROLLED
BY THE US

AREA
CONTROLLED
BY BRITAIN

AREA
CONTROLLED
BY FRANCE

LORCH

MAINZ

RIVER RHINE

The
FREE
STATE of
BOTTLENECK

This time, in the aftermath of World War I, the Allies had occupied German territory west of the Rhine. They got out their pairs of compasses, sharpened their little pencils and drew three circles—an American zone, a French zone[56] and a British zone—each with a radius of 19 miles, each centred on a nearby town.

Two of these towns—Mainz and Koblenz—were about 40 miles apart from each other. Very basic maths meant that the circles almost but didn't quite touch. And with the Rhine to the south and no roads to the mountainous north, a weird unloved strip of land found itself cut off from the rest of Germany. Somebody with an active imagination decided the shape looked a bit like that of a bottleneck, and so the Free State of Bottleneck was born. The largest town in the bottle, Lorch, was declared the capital.

But the sort of great powers who couldn't be bothered to draw maps properly certainly weren't bothered by what happened to a few thousand stranded Germans, and Bottleneck found itself unable to trade or do legitimate business with anybody, because officially it wasn't a thing. The populace was forced to make ends meet by smuggling and the odd train-hijacking. They issued an emergency currency, which featured a picture of locals having a much-needed drink. Sometimes they would moon the French troops garrisoned on their eastern border.

The Bottleneck technically came to end when the French decided to occupy the entire Ruhr valley—a response to Germany repeatedly defaulting on their World War I reparation payments—but, in 1994, some inhabitants of the former

---

[56] Just outside the Bottleneck, in the former French zone, you'll find the Mäuseturm, or "mouse tower," where a local legend claims the cruel and much despised Archbishop of Mainz was eaten alive by mice.

state tried reviving it, appointing ministers and even issuing passports. These are not recognised anywhere but do include a voucher that gets you a three-course dinner plus a discount on the locally produced wine.[57]

---

[57] Today, Lorch's exciting tourist attractions include a "Leprosy House" and a "Witches Tower." The Rhine Gorge, where the Bottleneck was situated, is now a UNESCO World Heritage Site. It has its own microclimate.

# THE TANGIER INTERNATIONAL ZONE
## 1924–56

POPULATION: CIRCA 150,000
CURRENCY: MOROCCAN FRANC, SPANISH PESETA, POUND STERLING
CAUSE OF DEATH: TOO LOUCHE
TODAY: PART OF MOROCCO
///SWINGING.MELON.WIDEST

If someone pointed a Bizarro ray at the whole concept of the nation state, then the Tangier International Zone is probably what you'd end up with. Not quite Europe, not quite Africa; not a country, not a colony; a marginal anything-goes airport lounge of a place. The perks included cheap cigarettes and three different postal systems to choose from. The drawback: more sleazy beat poets than you could throw a carpet at.

Like most port cities, Tangier had always been a bit sketchy. It lies only 20 miles from the Spanish coast—according to legend, Hercules tore the two continents apart as a favour to the North Africans. Samuel Pepys recorded his time there as "a hell of brimstone and fire" and called it "the excrescence of the earth." He complained that the city had no morals, which is rich coming from Mister Five-extramarital-affairs-a-day.

The International Zone was the result of Europe, as usual, not being able to agree on anything at all. Spain and France, the two big regional powers, both staked a claim to the city, and obviously Britain didn't want to be left out. In the end, France, Spain, Britain, Italy, Portugal, Belgium, the United States, Sweden and the Netherlands all agreed to "jointly administer" the 144-square-mile "interzone." The treaty they drew up agreed to a permanent neutrality, a police force no larger than 250 (enforcing only those laws shared by all the signatories) and "no games of chance." That last one seemed to get forgotten over the next few years. Beyond this vague semi-governance, it was a delinquent free-for-all.

Fashion designers, artists, loaded expats, spies, smugglers and arms dealers all bumped elbows at the cafés lining the Petit Succo. The smugglers liked it because, as a "free port," nothing could be considered contraband. The bohemians liked it because of all the drugs flowing in from the Rif mountains. Tangier was one of the few places in the world you could be openly gay without winding up in prison. The best thing was that, in a place without an identity, nobody had to think of themselves as a foreigner. Predictably, the feelings of the more local "Tangerinos" didn't register as a high priority.

The fabulously wealthy Barbara Hutton outbid Franco for a house there and proceeded to enjoy lots of vodka-based breakfasts.[58] In the evenings, she would throw decadent par-

---

[58] Barbara Hutton would phone up the American consul at all hours of

ties. The unhappy Woolworth heiress had her own grab bag of celebrity guests to choose from: Truman Capote, Cecil Beaton, Matisse, Ian Fleming, T.S. Eliot, Orson Welles and Tennessee Williams were all hanging about at some point or other. Nobody needed a work permit, and lots of writers moved there, but very few produced any actual work until they left again. William Burroughs (fresh off "accidentally" shooting his wife dead while attempting the William Tell apple trick) claimed that this was something to do with the spirit of the city, that the "air was slack," that everything had "a lack of vigour."[59] This is very much in the tradition of lazy writers blaming anything but themselves for failing to hit their word count.

When the French exiled the popular Moroccan king Mohammed V to Madagascar, the population began to riot. An upsurge of nationalism put the interzone on borrowed time: a debauched anti-country couldn't carry on inside the borders of a new Islamic nation state, even one as comparatively laid-back as Morocco.

the day to complain the Coca-Cola available in the international city didn't taste right.
[59] "Tangier"—Iain Finlayson

OTTAWA CIVIC HOSPITAL MATERNITY WARD
19 JANUARY 1943

POPULATION: 2, SORT OF
CAUSE OF DEATH: A BIRTH
TODAY: BACK TO BEING A BIT OF CANADA
///CAUTIOUS.SWAPS.TUBE

In the British comedy *Passport to Pimlico*, an unexploded bomb belatedly goes off in London, unearthing a document that reveals the streets above to be a long-lost part of the House of Burgundy.[60] Suddenly free from the United Kingdom's legal jurisdiction, and not subject to post-war rationing, a black market of illicit goods quickly springs up and things escalate from there. It seems like a fictional version of Cospaia, or maybe Neutral Moresnet, but in fact the film's screenwriter was inspired by an even more obscure bit of international territorial wrangling: a wartime hospital ward.

[60] The last ruler of the actual Duchy of Burgundy was Charles the Bold.

It is a stretch to call a maternity unit an extinct country, fair point, but as we've seen, definitions of nationhood are such a legal mess maybe we can just let this one slide. In 1940, Germany invaded the Netherlands, and the Dutch royal family went into exile. Princess Juliana fled to suburban safety in the Canadian capital, Ottawa. While living there, she got pregnant with her third child. This created a gigantic problem: the Dutch constitution was airtight on the issue—nobody could take their place in the line of succession if they were born on the soil of another country.

Contrary to popular belief, embassies—while having diplomatic immunity—are still territorially considered part of their host nation, so if you were thinking about getting your kid citizenship of a less terrible country than your own by having a baby in the Swedish ambassador's waiting room, forget it. Princess Juliana faced a dilemma, because obviously going back to the Nazi-controlled Netherlands wasn't an appealing option.

So, the Canadian government, and a number of high-powered lawyers, came to her rescue. They passed a law that would create an "extra-territorial" zone for the baby to be born in. A simple option might have been to earmark a particular place, but presumably that would have left open the possibility of the princess being out for a stroll, suddenly going into labour and the baby accidentally being born on Canadian soil after all. The wording of the proclamation solved this issue by providing "an extra-territorial character to any place in which the heir presumptive to the throne of the Netherlands may be confined and in which an heir to such throne may be born."

This amounted to a roaming bubble around the baby that became, in legal terms, a strange non-Canadian zone. It wasn't Dutch territory either, officially, though they did hang a big flag in the maternity ward, which itself happened to overlook Holland Avenue. The bubble was in effect a non-territory, a micro-sized repeat of the Tangier experiment (*see* page 118) in some ways, though with less in the way of bad poetry and hipster drug addicts.

At no point during the lengthy back-and-forth that led up to the proclamation did anyone turn round and say, "I don't know, are our entire concepts of nationhood and citizenship and the rules of royal succession . . . are they maybe a bit ludicrous?" Princess Margriet of the Netherlands was successfully delivered on 19 January 1943. If the pregnant Juliana had decided to murder someone at the exact moment of giving birth, it would have been an exciting legal grey area—but, perhaps distracted, she didn't take this opportunity. As a thank you to Canada, she later sent them 100,000 tulip bulbs.[61]

---

[61] If she'd given this gift 300 years earlier at the height of tulip mania, those 100,000 bulbs would have been worth 800,000 fat swine, 1,200,000 fat sheep, 400,000 tons of beer, 100 million pounds of cheese and 200,000 tons of butter.

LIES & LOST KINGDOMS

# The Great Republic of Rough & Ready
## 7 April–4 July 1850

POPULATION: CIRCA 3,000
CAUSE OF DEATH: ALCOHOL
TODAY: PART OF CALIFORNIA, USA
///SITUATED.DISPLAYING.INDECISION

Anywhere with "great" in the title is a bit dubious. It smacks of trying too hard. Raises the suspicion that maybe you're compensating for something. It's the personalised number plate of national nomenclature. In the case of Rough and Ready, the thing it's compensating for is almost certainly not being historically legitimate in the slightest, but that's not going to stop it from being in this book, because it's a daft story, and countries are just daft stories we tell each other. They're all equally implausible once you get up close.[62]

---

[62] Though there's arguably more excuse for this kind of hyperbole when you're a tiny mining community trying to make a name for yourself rather than, say, a sprawling empire who should know better.

In 1849 it was gold rush time in California, and a company of miners set up the outpost of Rough and Ready in the lucrative foothills of the Sierra Nevada, near a spot where an 18-pound gold nugget had been unearthed. It quickly turned into a little boomtown of 3,000 people. Life was good, in a hard working, hard drinking kind of a way, but trouble loomed. A new and predictably unpopular state-wide mining tax upset the independently-minded citizens. This was followed by a court case, where a local man, going by the honest-sounding name of "Joe Sweigart," felt he had been the victim of a grift carried out by a non-local, going by the much-less-honest-sounding name of "Boston Ravine Slicker."[63] When a judge ruled in the Slicker's favour Rough & Ready's populace decided enough was enough. California, on the cusp of becoming the 31st US state, wasn't doing much for them, so perhaps it was time to make their own rules. The town took a vote and decided to secede from the United States. Seceding from places had always been popular out west; it's how the States got going in the first place, and it played into the American myth of rugged individualism. In the middle of the nineteenth century, people would have seceded from pretty much anything if they thought it would get them a free hat.

They drew up a constitution (basically a find-and-replace job on the US one), made a flag,[64] appointed a retired colonel as president and went on their distinctive way. Which was

[63] The details of Boston Ravine Slicker's con are so weak that, if true, Sweigart deserved to get done over. Joe finds a seam of gold. Slicker bets him it's not that great and says he (Slicker) couldn't dig 200 dollars' worth of gold in a day. Joe takes up the bet. Judges are appointed. Slicker starts digging but then slows down as he nears 200 dollars' worth. Joe is somehow astounded by this clever "malingering" and loses the bet. The end.

[64] Rough and Ready's flag is not the flag of a country that deserves to exist.

fine, until they headed over to a nearby town[65] to buy liquor for the upcoming Fourth of July party. Their neighbours refused to sell them the booze on the grounds that they were now "foreigners." It was also pointed out that you couldn't really celebrate the Fourth of July if you weren't part of America anymore, could you?

The town promptly had another meeting. Everyone agreed rugged individualism wasn't all it was cracked up to be if you had to be sober doing it. And so, less than three months after they'd left, they voted to re-join California. Rough and Ready got to have its party.[66]

Supposedly, an ongoing dispute about the name of the town (the post office insisted it be called either "Rough" or "Ready," but not both) led to the discovery in 1948 that the paperwork readmitting the republic to the union had never been filed. The fact that this is almost certainly because there was never any paperwork to be filed in the first place, and that the whole doubtful episode is simply an excuse for a little town to put on an annual celebration and sell mugs to credulous tourists, is best ignored.

[65] Famous neighbour: Lola Montez, the Irish adventurer and dancer who almost brought down another extinct country (*see* Bavaria, page 26) briefly lived next door in Grass Valley.

[66] The twelfth US president, Zachary Taylor, nicknamed "Old Rough and Ready," didn't last much longer than the republic named after him, dying on 9 July 1850 after eating too much fruit.

CURRENCY: POYAIS DOLLAR (WORTHLESS)
CAUSE OF DEATH: CRUSHING REALITY
TODAY: PART OF HONDURAS AND NICARAGUA
///PUNCHLINE.MATERNALLY.THREADLIKE

One fun new Christmas tradition is the Very Disappointing Winter Wonderland. Each year, someone sells lots of expensive tickets to a Santa-based holiday extravaganza and it turns out to be a disused parking lot in Lubbock with a couple of ratty plastic trees and a trestle table with a solitary grumpy teen dressed as an elf, and everybody gets duly upset. The country of Poyais was the same deal—just scaled up a bit.

Gregor MacGregor (somehow his real name, one of the few genuine things about him) was yet another decorated war hero turned shady businessman. In 1821 he surprised London's high society by unexpectedly revealing that he was now the "Cazique" of a country called Poyais. The title had been bestowed on him by the king of the Mosquito Coast (the eastern portion of modern-day Nicaragua and Honduras). And Poyais? *What do you mean you haven't heard of Poyais? Perhaps you would care to read this 355-page guidebook, written by one Thomas Strangeways, who is definitely real and not a made-up pen name of me, Gregor MacGregor . . ."*

The guide—complete with illustrations—detailed this remarkable and hitherto-overlooked nation. It told of rivers in which chunks of gold regularly washed up. It told of natives who weren't just friendly but avidly Anglophile. There was a thriving port and city. Plans for an opera house. You could somehow harvest maize three times a year. And for the older members of the audience keen on getting their free pen, the moon was of such a special quality that "the smallest print is legible by her light."[67]

Investors and potential settlers were hurried along with "One Time Only, Grab It While Stocks Last" deals. It worked. MacGregor had picked his spot well: by the 1820s the Spanish Empire in South America was crumbling, and new nations were springing into existence. It was becoming a common thing for governments to raise funds in the City of London, and speculators were hungry for new opportunities. The only reason that Poyais hadn't cropped up on anyone's radar,

---

[67] He also produced a series of adverts and pamphlets written in the hyperactive style of the late, great Stan Lee. "POYERS! It shall be my constant study to render you happy!," "POYERS! Your future prosperity will be fully realised!'

MacGregor explained, was that a reluctance to antagonise the Spanish had stopped all its bountiful riches flowing out into the world. But now they were free to trade, and the sky was the limit.

He had another trick too: the bitter memories of the Darien fiasco a hundred years before (*see* page 80). Here was a chance for fellow Scots to put the shame of ill-fated New Caledonia behind them. MacGregor soon packed a boat with willing colonists: bankers, artisans, doctors, civil servants, everything you needed for a new society. The unfortunate rubes made the long journey across the Atlantic. When they arrived they found lots of impenetrably lush jungle. And nothing else. No buildings, no city, no chunks of gold floating in rivers, a suspiciously normal-looking moon. A second expedition arrived months later and found only the first set of suckers, miserable and half-dead from tropical diseases.[68]

The obvious question is: why did MacGregor feel the need to take his scheme to the crazy lengths he did? He'd already carried out a successful scam in Florida and done a runner with the proceeds. He could have tried the same thing here, exiting with the cash before anyone had to sail to their doom. Perhaps he really did have dreams of running his own country. The Mosquito King had genuinely, it seems, "given" MacGregor the territory—a whopping 12,500 square miles— in return for some "rum and trinkets." The fact that a promise and a piece of paper couldn't mean much fitted with the times: plenty of places had a similarly dubious start. Maybe he

---

[68] It is a measure of MacGregor's personal charm that when the setters found Poyais to be a big pile of nothing, they refused to blame him, instead pinning it on the "bad advice" he must have received.

thought the settlers might somehow make a go of it. Maybe he was a bit of a sociopath. Whichever it was, when news of the colonists' plight got back to London, his already shaky operation collapsed, and he hightailed it to France.[69] Where, obviously, he started the whole exact same ruse up again.[70]

[69] In terms of sheer size of fraud, only Bernie Madoff has managed to top MacGregor since.

[70] The French, a little more on the ball, arrested MacGregor. But he and his lawyer wrote a fictional 5,000-word character statement explaining what a great guy he was, and they ended up acquitting him.

# The Republic of Goust

POPULATION: <100
CAUSE OF DEATH: PROBABLY NOT EXISTING IN THE FIRST PLACE
TODAY: PART OF FRANCE
///SWEETENS.BORDERS.REFRESHMENT

G oust is the supposed microstate that didn't know it was a microstate. A single village, barely one square mile in size, located a thousand metres up a mountain near the border between France and Spain, it could only be reached by a narrow and precarious footpath that crossed the forbiddingly named *Pont d'Enfer*—BRIDGE OF HELL. The local population claimed remarkable longevity[71] (including several unverified centenarians) but, even so, they still tended to eventually die, same as the rest of us.

---

[71] Goust's claim to have had a resident live to 123 is doubtful. While the UN estimates there are well over 300,000 living centenarians in the world, only one person in history has been verified as having lived longer than 120.

Mountainous, out-of-the-way Goust did not lend itself to easy burial. The *Democratic Standard* newspaper of 1894 explained the solution:

> The pass which leads to the adjacent Spanish parish of Laruns is so steep that the carrying of heavy burdens is an impossibility. The inhabitants of this tiny mountain republic have built a chute, therefore, down which they slide heavy articles, and the bodies of their dead.

Rough & Ready's flimsy claim to nationhood might have been the result of wishful thinking on the part of the locals, but Goust's equally flimsy claim comes from a different source: the ever reliable press. Poorly researched "fake news" seems very modern and topical, but it's as old as the newspaper business. And a tiny country with a big slide to get rid of dead bodies is *exactly* the kind of thing that gets picked up by journalists looking to compile the nineteenth-century version of clickbait. Whilst the bizarre cadaver-chute at least seems to be true, Goust's status as a country is murkier.

The idea that Goust was never a part of France isn't entirely unreasonable: Charlemagne's empire bumping up against the Moorish Empire created lots of strange little buffer states between France and Spain. But Goust's independence myth seems to have stemmed from the French minister of the interior, in 1827, referring to it as "a republic"—but in an *entirely metaphorical fashion*. The newspapers then ran with that, and along the way forgot about the "metaphorical" bit. Goust became a minor sensation, even if the inhabitants never realized it. A trawl through the archives turns up dozens of articles mentioning "The Smallest Republic in the World!". Was it simply lazy reporting? Was it a deliberate attempt to jazz up an already quite weird story? In part Goust's brief fame has an even simpler explanation: newspapers have agendas, and they run stories that fit those agendas. The *Hawaiian Gazette*, for example, was preaching to an undersized kingdom that wasn't entirely sold on becoming part of the United States. That was all the incentive needed to put Goust on the front page, spinning an encouraging tale about how isolated, independent nations could successfully go it alone. Countries, it seems, aren't *just* daft stories we tell each other about ourselves: they're also the daft stories other people choose to tell about us.

If you want a semi-philosophical argument to consider: to all intents and purposes, somewhere as remote as Goust might as well have been an independent state, which is probably what the French minister was driving at in the first place. Like the proverbial tree falling over with no-one around to hear it, if people think a place is a republic—and that place is so cut off from the rest of the world that political changes elsewhere barely affect it—then do any of our legal definitions and categorizations even mean anything? Maybe. Possibly not. Have a biscuit.

Today, Goust has been made slightly, but only very slightly, more accessible by a road built 50 years ago. They no longer throw bodies down a chute.[72]

---

[72] These days there are more high-tech ways of disposing of bodies: you can have yourself liquefied, or your ashes pressed into a vinyl record. Some parts of Papua New Guinea and Brazil used to go with the extremely eco-friendly practice of endocannibalism. Tibet had the "sky burial"—i.e. being eaten by birds.

LIBERTALIA
IT'S TRICKY, BUT LET'S SAY 1707,
GIVE OR TAKE A FEW YEARS

LANGUAGE: A POLYGLOT, "THE DIFFERENT LANGUAGES BEGAN
   TO BE INCORPORATED, AND ONE MADE OUT OF THE MANY"
CAUSE OF DEATH: "A GREAT SLAUGHTER"
TODAY: PART OF MADAGASCAR
///BEACONS.FISHY.GOVERNABLE

He coasted along this Island to the Northward, as far as the most northerly Point . . . and on the Larboard-Side found it afforded a large, and safe, Harbour, with plenty of fresh Water. He came here to an Anchor, went ashore and examined into the Nature of the Soil, which he found rich, the Air wholesome, and the Country level . . . this was an excellent place for an Asylum.

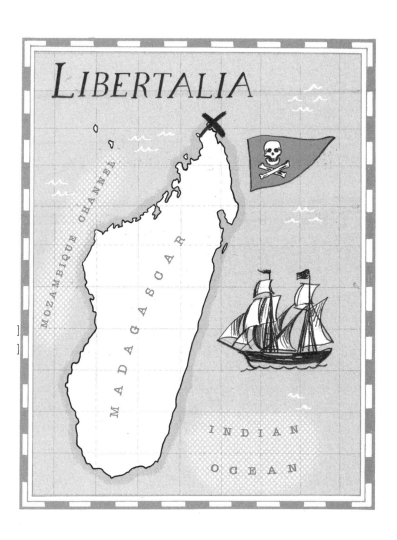

Captain Misson had already enjoyed a long and bountiful piratical career when he decided to found the socialist utopia of Libertalia on the northern coast of Madagascar. Originally from France, and oddly well-educated for a pirate—"a tolerable Mathematician," even—Misson had a reputation for fairness and wisdom. After attacking a Dutch slaver with his ship, the *Victoire*, he freed the slaves and declared that "the trading for those of our own Species, cou'd never be agreeable to the Eyes of divine Justice." Lots of pirates were comparatively egalitarian compared to the rest of the maritime world, but this was above and beyond.

Misson and his buccaneers arrived at Madagascar—about forty years too late to meet the last dodo on nearby Mauritius—and fortified the little bay they found. There, they set about building a new country, a place where everyone of any nationality or creed could peacefully coexist alongside the natives, no man deemed greater than another. They held democratic votes on important matters, set aside religion, constructed their own pidgin language and started doing a spot of farming.

Which sounds suspiciously fantastic. But if Rough and Ready's paperwork is a bit dubious, and Goust a confused journalistic mistake, Libertalia is (*almost* certainly) a flat-out lie. In 1724, the first edition of Captain Charles Johnson's *A General History of the Pyrates* appeared on the shelves of Charles Rivington's bookshop in the city of London. The author, supposedly a sailor himself, detailed the lives of several well-known historical pirates. The book's cover was boring, but the title was catchy, and so it sold well. Well enough that an expanded edition appeared a couple of years later. Which is where Misson—absent from the original text—suddenly turns up.

For a long time, the accounts were all taken at face value: Misson and his Libertalia were assumed to be as real as Bartholomew Roberts, William Kidd, Anne Bonny and Mary

Read. But where the other piratical biographies were at least in part verifiable, Johnson's book stubbornly remained the only source of information so far as Captain Misson was concerned. And Johnson himself seemed to be a figure who had sprung from nowhere.

Pirate havens certainly existed in places like Madagascar, but they were tough and impoverished and disease-ridden, nothing resembling the idyllic fantasy of Libertalia.[73] Gradually it became apparent that it was a work of fiction, albeit one that mixed a good amount of real history into the pot (though the fact that Captain Thomas Tew, a genuine pirate, turns up at Libertalia in 1707 despite having died in 1695 is possibly a bit of a giveaway).

By the 1930s, the finger of suspicion pointed at Daniel Defoe, always bendy with the truth and a man fond of a pseudonym.[74] The adventures of Captain Misson look a lot like the work of an author who, having run out of legitimate stories to tell but needing some new material to sate an eager public, decided to just make stuff up. Which, it is important to note, is very different to sticking an entirely fake nation in your book about genuine extinct countries.

[73] When Woodes Rogers, an English privateer who rescued the marooned Alexander Selkirk (inspiration for Defoe's *Robinson Crusoe*), sailed to Madagascar in order to research the pirates there, he found them to be "wretched."

[74] At one point in the twentieth century there was a bit of a fad to pin every work by an unknown author on Defoe, but there are several other candidates who could potentially be the mysterious Captain Johnson.

# The Kingdom of Sikkim
## 1642–1975

POPULATION: 200,000

CAPITAL: GANGTOK (PREVIOUSLY: YUKSOM, RABDENTSE, TUMLONG)

LANGUAGES: SIKKIMESE, CHOKE, LEPCHA, NEPALI

CURRENCY: PAISA

CAUSE OF DEATH: WRONG PLACE AT THE WRONG TIME

TODAY: PART OF INDIA

///WHIMPERED.HARDER.GEEK

In 1959, an American teenager called Hope Cooke found herself hanging out in Darjeeling's Windamere Hotel on the lookout for adventure,[75] One afternoon, over tea and cocktails, a man caught her eye, she caught his and Hope fell straight into what the press would describe as a Mills & Boon romance. And it would have been, if Mills & Boon had produced a *Doomed Geopolitical Nights: Screwed by Nixon* series.

[75] When Hope was still a little kid, her aviator mother crashed her plane in an apparent suicide—she'd not bothered to take enough fuel for the trip across Nevada.

The
KINGDOM of
SIKKIM

CHINA

NEPAL

TIBET

BHUTAN

GANGTOK

INDIA

The man was Crown Prince Thondup Namgyal, soon to be King of Sikkim, a romantic figure from a romantic country clinging on by its fingernails. Nobody quite knew what Sikkim was. When the British had first taken over great chunks of the globe, it suited them to engage in "manipulation without definition"—so long as the empire was making cash, then, honestly, who cared about the legal niceties? This fuzziness didn't matter until the subject of Indian independence came about, and suddenly all the murky deals and messy treaties presented a headache.

Beautiful mountainous Sikkim, with its snow leopards and its orchids, was one of the 600 princely states that should make up the new India—or was it? Historically, it had always been a place apart, Buddhist rather than Hindu, closer to the Tibetans than anyone else. Luckily for Sikkim, India's first prime minister, Jawaharlal Nehru, had some sympathy for the little state. It managed to stay in charge of its own destiny. But strategically squashed between Tibet, India, Nepal and Bhutan, every single superpower was now looking at it in the exact same way a hungry dog looks at a nice big ham.

When Thondup proposed to her, Hope was blissfully unaware of the tight spot she'd be marrying into. The idea of a young American queen didn't go down well. The local monks tried to delay the marriage by proclaiming the year inauspicious. A growing democratic movement within Sikkim already resented Thondup's authority and started to plant stories in the press about Hope being a CIA spy. (In fact, though she wasn't, both of Thondup's sisters were covertly ferrying notes to the Dalai Lama on behalf of the agency.)

The rest of the world thought the marriage was a fairy tale, but it got rocky fast. Thondup turned to drink. Meanwhile Hope got stoned, living on "consommé, bananas, valium and cigarettes." The kingdom was in an impossible position: the fickle geopolitical winds changed so fast it couldn't cosy up to one particular side even if it wanted to. Sikkim needed friends, but JFK and Nehru eventually gave way to Nixon and Indira Gandhi, and neither of those was someone you'd trust to look after a houseplant, much less the fate of your country. In a complete about-face, the United States suddenly started to court the Chinese. India, alarmed by this, had its own about-face and started to do deals with Russia. Tiny Bhutan was granted a seat at the UN, but Sikkim conspicuously wasn't.[76]

An increasingly miserable Hope unwisely took the piss out of Indira Gandhi's obvious ambitions towards her kingdom by sending out invites for parties at a non-existent "India House."[77] Thondup got drunker. In a plan to bolster the economy, the couple flew to New York to try to get a fashion line based on Sikkimese national dress off the ground. But the mood in the US press had chilled—instead of being the romantic dream of an American girl marrying royalty, Hope was now characterised as the Himalayan Marie Antoinette. Soviet disinformation mills, which were around a long time before Facebook, started to do their thing. Thondup's son was accused of plotting to kill the leaders of Sikkim's democratic movement by "dropping an explosive device in their vicinity." This was an exaggeration—it was actually a felt-tip pen.

When Indira Gandhi finally made her move, it was swift—it took 20 minutes and a single fatality for Indian troops to overpower the Sikkim guards. Thondup put out a plaintive distress call on his ham radio. Hope, having already fled her

[76] Hope bumped into the UN Secretary-General on a plane and tried to argue her country's case, but she'd taken a pill to calm her nerves and ended up garbling it.

[77] When Indira Gandhi was persuaded to visit Sikkim for a meeting about the country's future, a badly timed protest, featuring a lot of school kids holding a sign that read "WE ARE A BUFFER, NOT A DUFFER," didn't improve her attitude.

unhappy marriage for New York, suddenly found herself state-less, the citizen of a country that no longer existed. In order for her to be allowed to remain in America, the US Congress had to pass a special law just for her.

# The Kingdom of Axum
## circa 100–940

POPULATION: UNKNOWN
CAPITAL: AXUM (OR AKSUM)
LANGUAGE: GE'EZ
CURRENCY: GOLD, SILVER AND BRONZE COINS
CAUSE OF DEATH: A STRAINED ECONOMY, CLIMATE CHANGE, INVASION, OR MOST LIKELY A MIX OF ALL THREE
TODAY: PART OF ETHIOPIA
///MIMES.BOOKMARK.CORRODE

Because fashion is cyclical and Twitter is bad, Nazis are making quite the comeback right now. A sensible precaution would be to know where you could get hold of an ancient biblical super-weapon, just in case you need to melt their stupid Nazi faces off. There is a monk in Ethiopia who swears he has exactly that, the genuine, 100 per cent original Ark of the Covenant, but he definitely won't let you see it.

The
KINGDOM
of
AXUM

THE RED SEA

CITY
of
AXUM

(---- ROUGH TERRITORY AT GREATEST EXTENT)

For a lot of the West, Ethiopia and Eritrea mean famine and civil war, and if we bother to think about the region's history at all then we tend to skip 4 million years back to our most famous ancestor, Lucy the australopithecine. But this part of Africa was home to a kingdom that lasted the best part of a millennium—and which by the third century CE was one of the four great powers on the planet.[78]

Ethiopian tradition has it that Axum was founded by the son of King Solomon and the Queen of Sheba. Legendarily, the queen had a goat's hoof instead of a regular foot, because her mother, while pregnant, had stared covetously at a goat, "after the manner of women who are with child" (not a medically recognised fact). When she travelled from Ethiopia to visit him in Israel, Solomon had his floor polished until it was "as reflective as glass" in order to see if this rumour was true. Polishing your floor to surreptitiously look at women's legs apparently counted as "very wise" rather than "a bit much;" still, it was a different time back then, #notallprophets, etc.

In a convoluted tale, the queen goes home pregnant, her son Menelik grows up, visits his dad, semi-accidentally nicks the Ark and takes it back to Axum, where it remains to this day, in the Church of Our Lady Mary of Zion. A little conveniently, nobody is allowed to see the Ark except for one monk whose sole duty it is to look after it until he dies, and the job is passed

---

[78] When Italy invaded the city in the 1930s, for some weird reason the monks didn't use their anti-fascist weapon of mass destruction. The Italians stole one of the giant stelae and shipped it back to Rome, where it was erected as a monument to celebrate Benito Mussolini's fifteenth year in power. In 2005, after years of complaints, they finally took action to give it back, which proved tricky: it was too heavy to go via Ethiopia's roads, so it had to be loaded onto an Antonov An-124, the only plane big enough to lift it. Which itself could only land at the exact moment of dawn—there were no runway lights, so a night-time landing was impossible, and the air is so thin on the Ethiopian plateau that the plane would only be able to stay airborne when the temperature was below 60 degrees Fahrenheit.

to another. This sounds suspiciously like the kid at every school who claims to have that rare Pokémon/Star Wars figure/Lego Hogwarts but can't bring it in because it's at home behind some boxes and their arms are tired.

The problem is that the story doesn't match up with the archaeological record, which places the founding of Axum at about 100 CE, a full thousand years too late for Solomon. Even in vague prehistory terms, a thousand years is a pretty big miss. Though, before Axum there was the D'mt civilisation, about which we know very little, so possibly the two became conflated. Or possibly biblical archaeology is a mug's game because very little of anything ever matches up. What is certain is that Axum minted its own currency, expanded into the Arabian Peninsula, grew fabulously rich from trade and erected spectacular stone obelisks, known as "stelae," the skyscrapers of their day.[79]

The death of Axum is up for debate, though it seems likely the Axumites were victims of their own success: an ever-growing population had to farm more and more intensively in order to sustain themselves, especially once their trade network started to wobble. Soil erosion became catastrophic. Jared Diamond calls this kind of wilful short-termism "landscape amnesia"—"Didn't there used to be more trees and stuff here?" "Oh, it's fine, I'm sure it's always been like this"—the same thing that did for Easter Island. Climate change in the eighth century CE, when the rains started to falter, made things even worse. And, at some point, Axum simply became easy pickings for a warrior queen whose identity we can't ever be sure of.

[79] The tallest of the stelae still standing in Axum is 23 metres (five and a bit double-decker buses). The largest collapsed stelae is 33 metres.

# DAHOMEY
## CIRCA 1600–1904

POPULATION: 300,000 (IN 1700)
CAPITAL: ABOMEY
LANGUAGE: FON
CURRENCY: COWRY SHELLS
CAUSE OF DEATH: THE SCRAMBLE FOR AFRICA
TODAY: BENIN
///CHEEK.ROOSTERS.FUNKY

The Amazons of Greek myth were intended as a cautionary tale, a warning against messing with the patriarchal status quo.[80] "Look what happened to them! Extinct! That's what you get for role reversal and not sticking to gender norms! Pass me that papyrus, Socrates, I want to write an angry play about feckless millennials . . ." etc., and so on, down through the ages.

---

[80] Whether the original "mythological" Amazons existed is questionable, though archaeology has thrown up some evidence that they might have done, in the form of the Scythians.

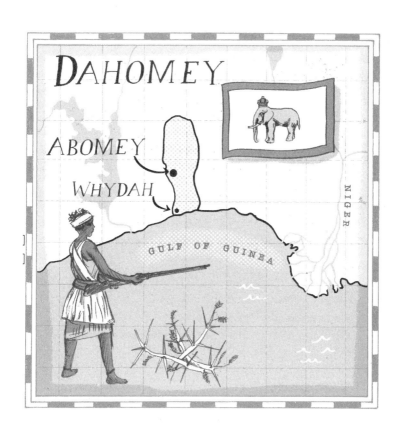

Dubiously motivated myths aside, we have a more recent, real-life version of the Amazons: the West African Kingdom of Dahomey,[81] unique for boasting a substantially female army. The origin of these warriors (or "Mothers," as they called themselves) is disputed. Like a lot of African history, it has to be filtered through the accounts of visitors who were racist, misogynist, sleazy or—most often—a charming combination of all three.

One story has the king of Dahomey praising his "wives" for a successful elephant hunt, and them responding that "a nice man-hunt would be even better." Another suggests that a depleted army was padded out with women to make it look bigger, but that those women then turned out to be much better soldiers than the men. What isn't disputed is that by the eighteenth century they numbered in their thousands, they were fierce and terrifying, and if needs be (according to one French observer) they "could tear apart a cow in less time than it would take a European abattoir."

Their harsh military training was typical of a country that seems to have enjoyed making life difficult for itself. The women would run through great big piles of two-inch-long acacia thorns. Then they'd do some "mime" fighting, which, like all mime, would have been annoying. After that, they'd run through another pile of thorns, just to prove a point. The reward for completing this would be a belt—which seems nice,

---

[81] Probably lies: Dahomey's name was supposedly a bad gag. Sometime around the early 1600s, the young King Dakodonu demanded a chunk of forest-savannah from a rival local chieftain. The chieftain, unimpressed, replied: "Should I open my belly and build you a house in it?" In an impressive demonstration of taking things much too literally, Dakodonu instantly disembowelled him and started to build a palace right there on his entrails, giving the new kingdom the name "Dahomey," which in the native language breaks down as *dan* ("chief,") *xo* ("belly") and *me* ("inside of.") Like all origin stories, this is almost certainly a crock, created to give later rulers a spurious legitimacy.

everyone likes a free belt, except the belts were made out of *a load more thorns*. Finally, they'd get to practise "insensitivity training" by throwing baskets of prisoners off high walls. One snooty early visitor criticised the women for shooting their imported vintage muskets from the hip, somehow missing the point that this is obviously the most stylish way to shoot your imported vintage musket.

It's important to note that Dahomey wasn't *entirely* some proto-feminist nation. The forcibly conscripted soldiers, some as young as eight, were technically all married to the king, and their main purpose—the main purpose of the whole country, really—was to help keep a booming slave trade ticking along. Every year Dahomey would go to war on some flimsy pretext (usually an imagined insult to the king's mother), but the real business was capturing human beings to sell, the hot commodity of the day.

"Black Sparta," as it came to be known in England, made its neighbours" lives hell for over a century and a half, but eventually Dahomey ran up against the colonising French, who had machine guns. Most of the "Amazons" were massacred in a series of bloody battles towards the end of the nineteenth century. Though a few warriors evaded death and then stealthily substituted themselves for the civilian Dahomey women already captured by the French soldiers—whose throats they then slit in their beds.

THE MOST SERENE REPUBLIC OF VENICE
697–1797


POPULATION: CIRCA 180,000 (BY 1490)
CAPITAL: VENICE
LANGUAGES: ITALIAN, VENETIAN
CURRENCY: VENETIAN DUCAT, LIRA
CAUSE OF DEATH: NAPOLEON
TODAY: PART OF ITALY
///SHRIMPS.BRIBING.PULP


In January 2018, four Japanese students sat down at a restaurant in Venice and ordered lunch. The bill came to 1,100 euros. When the story went viral, the Venetian tourist authorities pulled their best Claude-Rains-in-*Casablanca* faces—"I'm shocked—shocked—to find that people are being overcharged in this establishment!"—and slapped the restaurant with a steep fine to ensure it would never happen again. Six months later a nearby café hit the news when it charged a tourist 43 euros for two coffees and some water.

The
SERENE
REPUBLIC
of
VENICE

VENICE

A more honest reaction might have been a shrug and a wave towards Venice's glorious 800-year history of ripping people off. "I wrote you a long letter from Venice but the laudable love of gain . . . which burns with zealous heat in the breast of every Italian caused the hotel keeper to charge the postage and to throw the letter in the fire together with several others"— this was Mary Shelley complaining of being fleeced back in the nineteenth century.[82] Charging extortionate prices is what had made the city the most powerful maritime republic in the world.

It started off with salt. When their salt ponds flooded, the Venetians had to start importing it. The city paid well, and so local merchants eagerly sailed off to collect the stuff but, in the process, they brought other exotic items back with them. And quickly discovered that they could make a boatload more money acting as the middleman—buying low from the East and selling high to the West, or vice versa—than in producing the goods themselves.

Where other countries got side-tracked by religious and ethnic strife, the Serene Republic kept its eyes on the prize: naked capitalism.[83] The Venetians nobbled competitors. They set up some of the earliest banks. They sold the first coffee in Europe. Moneylenders, banned in most places, could operate in the city with impunity. The head of state, the doge, had all the usual spiritual trappings but was really the head of Venice

---

[82] Shelley's pal Lord Byron lived in Venice for three years, where he kept a creature menagerie including dogs, a wolf, a fox, some cats and a monkey.

[83] Unsurprisingly, this love of the bottom line went hand-in-hand with a dark underbelly. There was a widespread belief in witches and curses, one of which involved stealing someone's hair, wrapping it around a scorpion and burying it in some sand—as the scorpion died, so would the victim. The local Murano glass became popular in part because people thought it was sensitive to the presence of poison and would tremble or even shatter if any were poured into it.

Inc., presiding over an aristocratic boardroom. A merchant fleet of some 1,500 ships helped this country-shaped company to gradually expand as far as Padua, Vicenza and Cyprus. For the most part though, the republic grew not through conquest but sheer reliability. Venetian contracts were more dependable, and their networks better, than those of their competitors. Given the choice, they'd rather stay friendly with a neighbour—all the better to bleed their wallets.

The studied neutrality that was so great for business came back to bite them. When Venice tried to stay on good trading terms with Napoleon's France as well as his bitter enemy Austria, it only succeeded in annoying both sides. With 11 boats in Venice's official navy at this point, Bonaparte marched in unopposed, the panicking doge abdicated, and the republic was carved up by the Austrians and the French. Venice Inc found itself the victim of a hostile takeover.[84]

[84] "A man without money is a corpse who walks"—old Venetian proverb.

# THE GOLDEN KINGDOM OF SILLA
## 57 BCE–935 CE

POPULATION: 2 MILLION (IN THE EIGHTH CENTURY)
CAPITAL: GYEONGJU
LANGUAGE: OLD KOREAN
CURRENCY: OSHUCHON
CAUSE OF DEATH: AN OBSESSION WITH CLASS
TODAY: PART OF NORTH AND SOUTH KOREA
///BACHELOR.SINGERS.CONGA

As origin stories go, it's not totally convincing. Villagers see an eerie light one evening and head off to investigate. They find a giant red egg, out of which hatches a bouncing baby with a "radiant visage." The glowing infant is anointed as a future monarch, the first of a line that will last for centuries. A kingdom is born. Nearby animals start to dance, Disney-style.

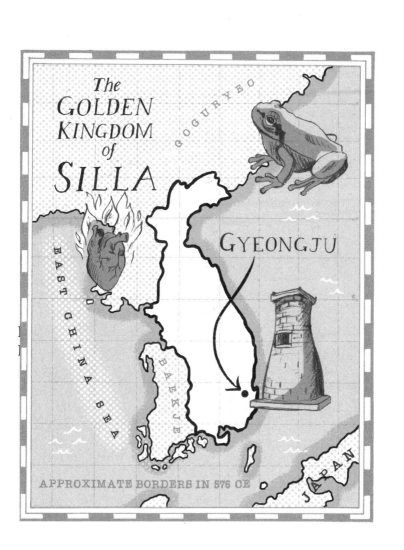

The GOLDEN KINGDOM of SILLA

GOGURYEO

GYEONGJU

EAST CHINA SEA

BAEKJE

JAPAN

APPROXIMATE BORDERS IN 576 CE

Historians tend not to accept egg-based explanations for the birth of countries, and a more likely story is that Silla (literal meaning: "encompassing the four directions by its virtuous achievements") evolved from one of 12 city states that dominated the Korean peninsula 2,000 years ago. Well-stocked burial mounds tell us that the kingdom gradually grew an extensive trading network—stretching as far as the Middle East—and that the citizens of Silla really liked whacking great piles of gold (hence the bling "golden kingdom" nickname), but beyond that the details get vague. One thing we do have is a fairly complete list of the kingdom's rulers, which is where Silla managed an inadvertently progressive achievement.

The kingdom based its entire society on "bone rank." Like a royal bloodline, but more extreme, your bone rank dictated the colours you wore, the maximum dimensions of your house, your job, and pretty much everything else. The top rank—Sacred Bone—meant that you were descended from the royal line on both sides. Beneath that was True Bone (bit shabbier—one side royal, one side noble). And after that a variety of non-bone ranks of diminishing importance. Only those from the Sacred Bone caste could sit on the throne.

This ultra-rigid hierarchy ran into a problem halfway through the seventh century when there were suddenly no more Sacred Bone males left. The country had to choose between having a female ruler (not a thing this part of the world had even considered back then) or lowering the entry requirements. They decided gender mattered *slightly* less than class, and so, in 632 CE, Seondeok, daughter of King Jinpyeong, was crowned queen.

Said to be wise enough to predict the arrival of an enemy army because she'd "seen some frogs," she was also so beautiful that when she met a peasant with an unrequited crush on her, his heart exploded into flames—burning down a royal pagoda, which is the kind of embarrassing social death we can all identify with. Myths aside, by 643 CE Silla found itself besieged. The peninsula was divided into three warring kingdoms: Silla, Baekje and Goguryeo. Queen Seondeok sent an envoy to China, to ask the Tang emperor for help. Emperor Taizong's reply was a patronising mansplain: it seemed obvious, he argued, that things were out of balance in Silla. The heavenly principles of the hard male yang and the soft female yin meant any right-thinking person would realise that women were subordinate, and this was why Silla's enemies were giving it such grief. A solution, Taizong went on to suggest, might be for him to send a man over to rule in Seondeok's place?

To Seondeok's credit, she somehow refused this idea politely enough that the alliance was later agreed, and over the subsequent few years Silla successfully conquered its two rivals, unifying the Korean peninsula for the first time.[85] Moreover, Seondeok achieved the ultimate accolade for any great leader—she made it into *Civilization VI* (well, the expansion pack—still counts), which is something Taizong never managed.[86]

---

[85] Seondeok also built the first dedicated astronomical observatory in the Far East—Cheomseongdae, which still stands today. Though, because it predates telescopes by a thousand years, the actual observatory element is basically "a hole to look out of."

[86] Silla had two subsequent queens, until the nobility decided that maybe keeping women in their place was more important than class after all and let the Sacred Bone requirement slide. The rest of the bone rank system remained in place. The increasing frustration this caused at all levels of society, kept from advancement by their birth, probably contributed to the kingdom's fall after a thousand years, when it splintered back into three separate kingdoms.

# KHWAREZMIA
## 1212–20 (IN ITS FINAL FORM)

POPULATION: 5 MILLION
CAPITAL: VARIOUSLY: GURGANJ, SAMARKAND, GHAZNA AND TABRIZ
LANGUAGES: PERSIAN, KIPCHAK
CURRENCY: DRACHM
CAUSE OF DEATH: A TOTAL LACK OF MANNERS
TODAY: IRAN, UZBEKISTAN, AFGHANISTAN AND TURKMENISTAN, ROUGHLY
///SLIPPERS.SPONGE.PORRIDGE

Passports are important. Some people will go to insane, nation-crippling lengths just to ensure they're the correct colour. Genghis Khan took them even more seriously. One surviving example of a Mongol passport, a small metal disc, reads: "I am the emissary of the Khan. If you defy me you die." Another is even more succinct—"LET PASS OR DIE!" If you were ruling a country back in the thirteenth century and a guy turned up carrying one of these, then you would have to be a colossal idiot to ignore that warning.

Shah Ala ad-Din Muhammad was that colossal idiot.

Of all the deceased countries in this book, it's hard not to feel Khwarezmia had it coming. Covering a large chunk of Asia, the shah's empire rivalled Genghis's in size, if not in organisational nous. Relations between the two were frosty from the start. But in an out-of-character move, Genghis came looking for peace and trade, having had his fill of pillaging absolutely everything he could see. He sent Muhammad a friendly note: "I am the sovereign of the sunrise and you are the sovereign of the sunset." While geographically accurate, this could also be read as a not-very-subtle diss and didn't go down well.

Muhammad sent Genghis a slightly crap present of some silk—the equivalent of the time Obama awkwardly gifted Gordon Brown a box of DVDs. Privately, Genghis was sniffy—"Does the man imagine we've never seen stuff like this?"—but he didn't let on. He dispatched an envoy, Mahmud Yalavech, with a huge gold nugget, and an oral message that this time referred to the shah as "my son." This also failed to go down well. The shah accused Yalavech of being a spy, but Yalavech fast-talked his way out of it, flattering him with tales of how tiny and useless the Mongol army was compared to the forces of Khwarezmia. Muhammad let the envoy go but continued to secretly seethe.

Then a huge Mongol trading caravan turned up in the city of Otrar. Over 400 merchants with 500 camels and another 100 cavalry. The caravan sought to get Khwarezmia to lift an embargo on cloth (Mongolia had a cloth shortage, which is serious when your entire civilisation is tent-based).

Muhammad didn't lift the embargo. In fact, he went slightly further than that: he ordered every last one of the merchants killed, once again accusing them of being spies.[87] One man,

---

[87] In addition to the ludicrous "spies" claim, the shah also moaned that he

who happened to be taking a bath at the time, managed to escape the massacre. He fled back home to report it. Unbelievably Genghis Khan, not a man famous for his "live and let live" attitude, took the news in his stride and offered the shah a diplomatic get-out. He dispatched a party of three to explain his proposal: declare it was all "a demented mistake" on the part of the city's governor, hand him over and everything would be fine. The shah responded . . . by killing the head of the mission on the spot and sending the other two back with their beards burned off. At about this point, an ambassador turned up to let the shah know his research suggested that actually this Genghis man and his Mongols were absolutely not to be messed with. The shah presumably pulled a "whoops" face. Genghis's next message was to the point: "You kill my men and my merchants and you take from them my property. Prepare for war, I am coming against you with a host you cannot withstand."[88]

had been addressed by the wrong title, which hints at what a touchy brat he was.

[88] The shah proved no better at war than he was at diplomacy. He hid at the back of badly controlled troops because he'd been spooked by the predictions of his astrologer. Unlike most astrologers, this one was right on the money: Khwarezmia was toast.

PUPPETS & POLITICAL FOOTBALLS

# THE REPUBLIC OF FORMOSA
## MAY–OCTOBER 1895

POPULATION: < 3 MILLION
CAPITAL: TAIPEI
LANGUAGES: TAIWANESE, FORMOSAN, HAKKA
CURRENCY: QING DYNASTY COINAGE
CAUSE OF DEATH: HOPELESS PRESIDENTS, JAPAN
TODAY: NOW TAIWAN, OFFICIALLY PART OF THE REPUBLIC OF
   CHINA
///SEARCHER.DEFECTORS.MISNAMED

Some nation states—even massive ones like China—are so weirdly insecure that they get anxious if, say, your contents list happens to contain the name of a country they don't officially recognise as ever having existed. To the extent that they'll refuse to print your book and you'll have to go and get it done in Slovenia instead.[89]

---

[89] Slovenia, being part of the Balkans, inevitably has a slightly more adult level of acceptance about the confusing nature of existence than the One Indivisible China.

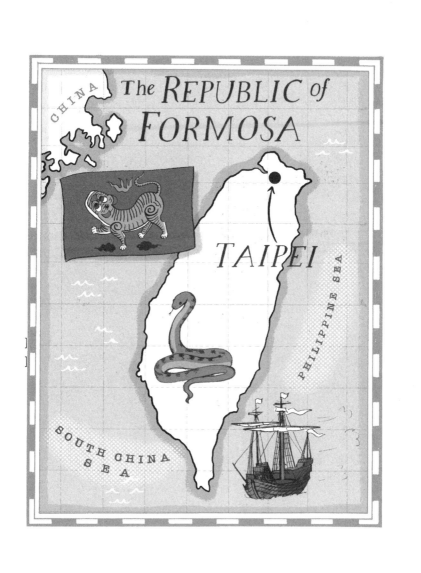

The irony here is that we're not talking about the perennial hot potato of Tibet, but about a republic whose sole aim was to *remain* a part of China—the exact opposite of the island's political struggles today.

The name "Formosa" dates from the mid-sixteenth century, when a Portuguese trading vessel, blown off course by a typhoon, sailed past the island's eastern coast. One of the crew, struck by the impressive landscape, referred to it as Ilha Formosa ("beautiful island") and the name stuck. Later it became a Dutch colony, and then a part of the Chinese empire. In the West it briefly hit the headlines when the Frenchman George Psalmanazar published *An Historical and Geographical Description of Formosa* (1704), detailing the island's bizarre customs. London society lapped up his lurid descriptions of how Formosans, who spent all their time naked, lived off a diet of serpents, and of how the men would eat their wives if they were unfaithful, all while priests sacrificed 18,000 young boys *every year*. Plus, everyone lived underground in huge circular houses. It is important to note that every single thing in Psalmanazar's book is bullshit.[90]

In real life, by the late nineteenth century Formosa was struggling. A backwater of the Chinese empire, it attracted the calibre of administrator who today you'd find running a privatised train company. Corruption and inefficiency were endemic. And the mainland wasn't doing so well itself. China and Japan had gone to war over Korea, and China had lost badly. The Treaty of Shimonoseki was the humiliating peace Japan forced upon them—demanding, among other things, Formosa.

[90] Psalmanazar tried the same trick when he first turned up in England by recounting equally unlikely stories of his travels in Ireland, but he found a few too many people already knew what Ireland was like. Perhaps most impressively, he even managed to teach a totally made-up Formosan language at Oxford University.

The leader of the Chinese delegation tried to persuade Japan that they didn't *really* want it, arguing the island was riddled with malaria and opium addiction. Japan saw through this brilliant ploy and stuck to their guns. A date was set for handing the territory over. Predictably, a lot of the Formosans felt badly sold out by the motherland, and the local elites rebelled. The reluctant governor, T'ang, issued a declaration of independence: "the literati and people of Formosa are determined to resist subjection by Japan. Hence they have declared themselves an independent island republic, at the same time recognising the suzerainty of the sacred Tsing [Qing] dynasty." There was a misplaced hope that the British would step in to protect this plucky new nation against the Japanese invaders. Again, who knows where anyone got that idea, because this is not, very obviously, how the British tend to operate.

When the first contingent of Japanese troops turned up, the self-proclaimed government instantly fled, leaving an angry mob to set fire to their offices. T'ang himself visited a port on the pretext of conducting a military inspection, and then simply hopped onto a departing German boat. This led to his nickname, "the Ten-Day President."

A small Japanese army unit took the capital in one day, but the south of the island put up a slightly tougher resistance. A successful general called "Black Flag" Liu was (again reluctantly) named the new president. He tried to start up negotiations with the Japanese, but they were in no mood to talk. Before long, president number two was also making his escape to the mainland, this time dressed in rags and disguised as a refugee. After 500 people were killed in two days of anarchic mayhem, most of the merchants and shop owners were ready to welcome the Japanese takeover—because, they reasoned, it couldn't go much worse than the last two guys' efforts.

The legacy of the short-lived republic is an odd one. Despite being an attempt to remain a part of China, the flag is now a rallying point for those seeking independence (mainly because it's such a great flag, a happy lion who looks like a very good boy). And the experience seems to have left the Taiwanese wise to the fact that, when push comes to shove, neither China nor anyone else is looking out for them.

# The Republic of West Florida
## September–December 1810

CAPITAL: St. Francisville
CURRENCIES: Spanish colonial real, US dollar
CAUSE OF DEATH: swallowed by the United States
TODAY: part of Louisiana
///DELIVER.TRENDY.PENNILESS

The gate of Fort San Carlos had been left open, so the band of 50 revolutionaries who had assembled outside it that morning simply wandered in. One minute later, after a half-hearted exchange of gunfire with the Spanish soldiers inside, their unexpectedly easy revolution was over. They seized the fort and unfurled a flag to announce the birth of the Lone Star State. No, not *that* one, the proper one: the Republic of West Florida.

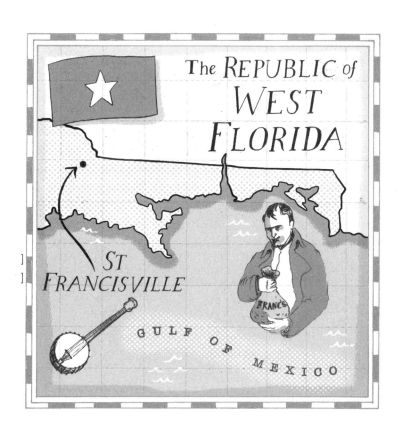

It's important to point out that while the original Lone Star State wasn't Texas like everyone thinks, it wasn't Florida either. This is because, confusingly, the Republic of West Florida was in what is now Louisiana.[91] One of the reasons it's confusing is because everything in America was confusing at the start of the nineteenth century. In 1803, across the Atlantic, Napoleon had a cash-flow problem. Trying to take over Europe is expensive. He offered the fledgling United States a deal: the Louisiana Purchase. In the bargain of the century, the States paid 50 million francs and got a chunk of French territory that stretched from the south in New Orleans to as far north as Canada, and from Wyoming in the west to Iowa in the east.

Fly in the ointment: it wasn't totally clear whether France owned everything it was selling. Spain claimed that, back when it had first ceded the region to the French, one small area hadn't been included—a strip of land between Baton Rouge and just east of Pensacola. The United States disagreed, but they weren't keen to provoke a war. So, the disputed area, despite an influx of Americans, continued on under the rule of Spain. That was okay for a while, but the West Floridians, or at least some of them, found the Spanish administration increasingly corrupt.

This group of would-be revolutionaries began to plot. Melissa Johnson (the wife of the cavalry officer tasked with leading the revolt) designed a flag of independence: a single white star on a blue background.[92] They marched on the fort.

---

[91] Extra confusingly, there was also something called the Republic of the Floridas, declared a few years later. Which also began with a group of soldiers seizing a Fort San Carlos, though a different Fort San Carlos, over on Amelia Island on the east coast. This republic didn't come to anything, because the man behind it was the future Cazique of Poyais (see page 132), Gregor MacGregor, up to his usual tricks.

[92] The legacy: the republic didn't only bequeath a flag to the independent Texas, it also helped kick off the whole "Manifest Destiny" fad (see page 46).

After their slightly anticlimactic 60-second victory, the republic lasted another 78 days under the leadership of the excellently named Fulwar Skipwith. Then the United States quietly swallowed it up, all without having to lift a finger. But West Florida didn't die before the inhabitants came up with an anthem that referred to the country as "Floriday" just so there was something to rhyme with "Tyranny," which is poor lyric writing however you cut it.

# MANCHUKUO
## 1932–45

POPULATION: 35 MILLION
CAPITAL: HSINKING, TONGHUA
LANGUAGES: JAPANESE, MANCHU, MANDARIN
CURRENCY: MANCHUKUO YUAN
CAUSE OF DEATH: WORLD WAR II
TODAY: PART OF CHINA
///BICKER.CREW.POWDER

In the middle of the nineteenth century, Japan woke up from a self-imposed slumber, blearily rubbed its eyes, looked around at all the appalling things the Europeans were getting away with and said: "Think you guys are bad? Hold my Asahi, you colonialist bastards, we'll show you how it's done."[93]

---

[93] To be fair, Japan rightly realized that they were now faced with a choice: get busy throwing their weight around or face the same unhappy fate as everyone else the Europeans had dealings with.

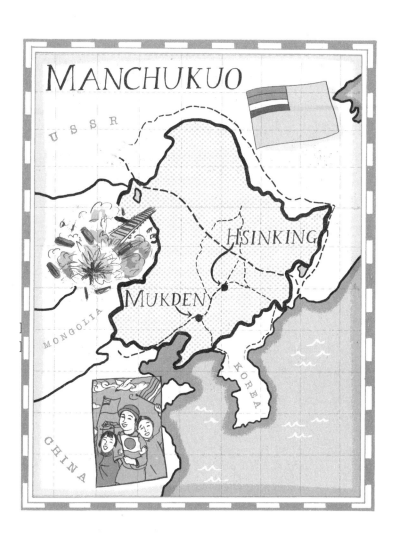

Within fifty years they'd already fought a war in Korea and grabbed Formosa from China, but that didn't sate their new expansionist thirst. Further opportunity came in the form of a train. In the late 1800s, the Russian tsar had travelled across his vast empire and decided he fancied being able to do it in a bit more style, ideally something with a dining car and a personal chef—so he resolved to complete the Trans-Siberian Railway. Impatient to get the job done, the engineers took the most direct route, which involved a shortcut across China.[94]

Before long, it was Russia and Japan's turn to come to blows. The brief war and subsequent peace treaty saw Japan take over this Chinese portion of the Russian railway. Officially, it had only won control of the narrow South Manchuria Railway Zone, as it was known, but it was soon building settlements along the route. This creeping expansion of its territory didn't creep fast enough as far as the Japanese government was concerned. It needed an excuse to speed things up.

These days, nothing happens in the world without some bonkers part of the internet screaming "FALSE FLAG OPERATION!!" Back in 1931, it was still a relatively novel trick. The Japanese blew up a small chunk of their own railway and blamed it on "Chinese terrorists."[95] That was all the pretext they needed. The rest of the world instantly saw through the scheme because it was rubbish.[96] The League of Nations got

[94] Russia was allowed to build the "Chinese Eastern Railway" across Manchuria because of a concession granted by the faltering Qing dynasty, who weren't in a position to say no to much of anything at this point (*see* page 54).

[95] Prior to Manchukuo, the Japanese had already blown up a train to get rid of an irritating Chinese warlord, so it was something they'd had a bit of practice at.

[96] Probably lies: the rumour that the Vatican was one of the countries that recognised Manchukuo, popularised by Bertolucci's *The Last Emperor*, is false, though it did send an envoy.

showily upset—and totally failed to act. The army moved in and the country of Manchukuo was unveiled.

It started as a fake republic and then morphed into a fake kingdom. Japan tapped the last Emperor of China as a figure-head, lending it some spurious legitimacy. All countries are huge PR exercises to an extent and Manchukuo was no different, though the PR was so over the top, and so much the antithesis of what was happening, that today it comes across as a very dark joke. Posters of rosy-cheeked multicultural children popped up everywhere. One book designed to show "everyday life" had a photograph of a family with the caption "a member of the Manchukuo intelligentsia voluntarily posing for a picture with his wife and two children." Hint for future puppet regimes trying to seem legit: leave out the word "voluntarily," it's a bit of a giveaway.

Beneath the cheery facade, unwanted ethnic minorities were being wiped out with chemical weapons. Unit 731 conducted human experimentation worse than anything even the Nazis managed, all under the sunny-sounding title of "the Epidemic Prevention and Water Purification Department." Japan's new hyper-nationalism inevitably led to its puppet state getting into another tangle with the Russians. This time things didn't work out so well: the Soviets invaded Manchukuo with precision timing, two days after Hiroshima.

# THE RIOGRANDENSE REPUBLIC
## 1836–45

POPULATION: CIRCA 350,000
CAPITALS: PIRATINI, ALEGRETE, CACAPAVA DO SUL, BAGE, SAO
  BORJA
LANGUAGE: PORTUGUESE
CURRENCY: BRAZILIAN REAL
CAUSE OF DEATH: JERKY PRICES
TODAY: PART OF BRAZIL
///WALTZ.BOGGLE.LOUDMOUTH

A lot of would-be nations had, at their hearts, something that looks inconsequential. Rough and Ready objected to the Californian mining tax. The town of Menton declared independence after Monaco tried to squeeze them with a lemon tax (if you're a lemon fan you can still visit their annual lemon festival, full of colossal sculptures made entirely out of lemons). For the gauchos of South America, the pet beef was beef jerky.

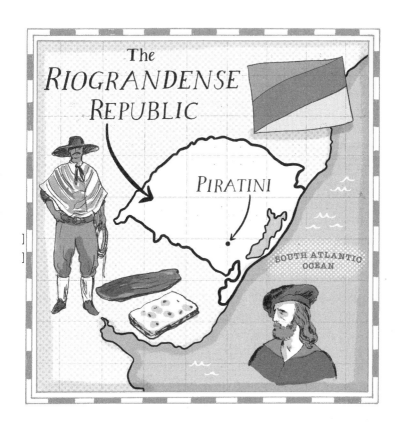

The
*RIOGRANDENSE*
REPUBLIC

PIRATINI

SOUTH ATLANTIC
OCEAN

Pedro I, Emperor of Brazil, came from one of those difficult families where Christmases are incredibly awkward. He'd
already fought a successful war of independence against his
own father, the king of Portugal. When his dad's death resulted
in Pedro becoming ruler of both countries, he abdicated the
Portuguese throne in favour of his daughter Maria so that he
could concentrate on running Brazil. At which point his
younger brother promptly usurped her. Pedro headed back to
Europe to sort out this latest bit of domestic strife, abdicating
the Brazilian throne in favour of his son.

Pedro II was only five, and five-year-olds aren't known for
their diplomacy skills, so Brazil found itself in a delicate situation. Power vacuums tend to magnify existing grievances. The
gauchos were a group with a grievance. Gauchos are basically
the South American version of cowboys: tough and unruly and
fond of a good horse. They controlled the huge sweeping
grasslands of the Rio Grande do Sul province, almost half the
size of France, where they made their living raising cattle and
producing tons of beef jerky.[97] Cheaper jerky imports from the
rest of South America had started to flood the market, leaving
the gauchos unhappy with their lot. There was some unkind
name-calling: the gauchos referred to the Brazilian royalist
government as "camels." The royalists referred to the gauchos
as "ragamuffins" (because of the raggedy nature of their outfits). And so began the Ragamuffin War.

"Establishing a republic" is a better rallying cry than "being

---

[97] How to make beef jerky: Cut your choice of steak (flank steak is good)
into thin strips one-eighth of an inch thick. Slice with the grain for chewier
jerky. Marinate as you see fit, with pepper, salt, soy sauce, Worcestershire
sauce, etc (mix it all in a bowl and then leave your jerky in the marinade in
the fridge for at least a few hours). If you don't own your own dehydrator,
lay the jerky out on a wire rack (over a baking tray) and cook at 175 degrees
Fahrenheit for about three hours. Turn over the jerky and cook for another
three hours.

angry at cheap foreign jerky," so that's what the uprising pretended to be about. Luck would have it that a lot of Italian would-be republicans were mooching around Rio having noisy "secret" meetings. They'd gather in cafés and hold earnest student-y conversations about political theory. One of them, a young Giuseppe Garibaldi, bored of the endless discussions, favoured more direct action. A meeting with one of the captured Ragamuffin leaders while visiting a jail persuaded him to join their cause.

Although it was 40 years before Garibaldi mania would see biscuits named in his honour and little porcelain figurines of him for sale in all the best London shops, he was already a brilliant military strategist. Together with his equally daring lover Ana, he led the small gaucho navy to an unlikely victory. On 11 September 1836, the Riograndese Republic proclaimed itself independent from the empire of Brazil, though the ongoing war and the itinerant nature of the gauchos meant it moved capitals five times in the space of its nine-year existence. But to the Italian revolutionaries' disappointment, the gauchos didn't really care about lofty republican ideals. As soon as Brazil agreed to protect their jerky profits, self-interest won out and the Riograndese government and country collapsed peacefully back into the empire. If he wanted to start a country, Garibaldi was going to have to do it somewhere else.

# MARYLAND IN AFRICA
## 1834–57

POPULATION: < 1100
CAPITAL: HARPER
LANGUAGES: ENGLISH, GREBO
CURRENCY: US DOLLAR
CAUSE OF DEATH: FAMINE AND UNFRIENDLY NEIGHBOURS
TODAY: PART OF LIBERIA
///UNSOCIABLE.OPTIMIST.ELBOW


There were two types of white people in the US state of Maryland in the 1830s, the really racist ones and the not-quite-as-bad-but-still-let's-face-it-fairly-racist ones. The really racist ones were pro-slavery. The not-quite-so-racist ones were anti-slavery but worried that former slaves would inevitably Get Up to No Good. The idea both groups hit upon was simple: wouldn't it be great if all the people of colour could be persuaded to go and live somewhere else? Africa, perhaps . . .

HARPER

SIERRA LEONE

LIBERIA

FRENCH WEST AFRICA

MARYLAND in AFRICA

For the most part, the black Marylanders weren't keen on this plan. Partly because Africa was thought to be a place of snakes and cannibals, and partly because the former slaves very fairly reasoned that having lived in the new world for several generations, they were every bit as American as their white neighbours. Even so, the newly formed Maryland State Colonization Society (an offshoot of the already-established American Society for Colonizing the Free People of Colour of the United States) managed to persuade a small group to set sail for the West African coast. It's hard to blame those who took the offer up, because being a freed slave was almost as bad as slavery at this point: you had no rights, no vote and almost certainly no job. The boat hired by the society was covered in barnacles and the captain was a drunk, but like all colonists, those on board had dreams of a better life.

The colony of Liberia had already been established some years before as a home for freed American slaves, but the Maryland society decided to go it alone. Dr. James Hall was the brains behind the operation. An ill man who was escaping treatments including "antiphlogistic therapy" (in which inflammation in one part of the body is supposedly reduced by irritating another part, an inexplicably popular remedy at the time), he pored over his maps and finally identified the fertile-looking spot of Cape Palmas as a good location for the new Maryland.

Despite the drunk captain and the barnacles, the colonists survived the voyage and Dr. Hall went to sit down for a "palaver" with King Freeman, representative of the local population, the Greboes. They haggled over the price the settlers would pay for the land. The traditional way of looking at these encounters is to see wily Westerners ripping off naive natives. But it's not clear who was playing who. Previous would-be settlers in the region had also offered goods in exchange for the land. Invariably, these strangers had found the place too tough and hostile, given up and gone home. The Greboes possibly figured there was a good chance of history repeating itself. So why not winkingly "sell" their land, seeing as it would only be a temporary deal?[98]

Sure enough, the colonists struggled. Their houses had leaky roofs and muddy floors. The mangrove swamps were malarial.[99] They relied upon the locals for food, but the recent harvests had been so bad there wasn't any. When they tried to farm their land, they found their crops failed miserably. Most subsisted on a diet of cabbage palm and potato leaves. A dispute over the price of sheep led to a violent uprising. Dr. Hall tried to intervene to stop the locals conducting their witchcraft trials, which didn't go down well. And it turned out that King Freeman wasn't king of everything he'd claimed.

When Liberia announced independence from the American Colonization Society in 1847, Maryland did the same, but the declaration didn't mean a whole lot. Famine loomed. Disputes with the Greboes over the land got worse and bloodier. It became clear that the country couldn't stagger on much longer without help. In 1857, the surviving colonists quietly voted to be swallowed up by their neighbour for their own protection.

---

[98] Initial native demands for their land: 20 puncheons of rum, 20 cases of guns, 20 barrels of powder, 20 bales of cloth, 20 brass kettles, 20 boxes of hats, 20 boxes of cutlasses, 20 boxes of beads, 100 iron pots, 20 cases of looking glasses, 100 dozen red caps, 200 iron bars, 20 knives, 20 crates of wash basins, 20 hogsheads of tobacco, 1 box of umbrellas, 100 boxes of pipes, 20 kegs of flints, 2 boxes of large copper wire, 2 gross of spoons, 3 gross of forks, 100 tumblers, 100 bottles of wine, 20 boxes of soap, 10,000 fish hooks, 100 tin pails, 100 stone jugs, 20 demijohns, 20 cases of snuff boxes, 20 boxes of candles, 2 cases of bells, 20 suit cloths, 3 beds and bedsteads, 6 boxes of cloth, 3 cock'd hats, 6 epaulettes, 3 dozen flags (source: Hall, 2003).

[99] Dr. Hall was about 60 years ahead of his time with his use of "sulphate of quinine" to ward off malaria, though he had no clue how it worked. Medical science of the time blamed the disease on the mangroves rather than the mosquitoes.

A grim postscript in case the story isn't already grim enough for you: the Bridgestone Corporation, which operates as Firestone in Liberia, was found guilty of forced labour by the UN as recently as 2005. Modern-day slavery goes on flourishing in the state set up for free slaves.

# The Republic of Texas
## 1836–46

POPULATION: > 140,000 (BY 1847)
CAPITALS: TOO MANY
LANGUAGES: ENGLISH, SPANISH, FRENCH, GERMAN, COMANCHE
CURRENCY: THE TEXAS "REDBACK" DOLLAR
CAUSE OF DEATH: IT DIDN'T REALLY WANT TO EXIST IN THE FIRST PLACE
TODAY: PART OF THE USA
///MONDAY.PREOCCUPIED.GANGS

When the Brexit results were announced, a small group in Texas got very excited. If the fey, famously reticent limeys could risk their economy collapsing for the sake of some semi-mythical nostalgia then surely the comparatively bold "Texians" could too. The press even started referring to "Texit," because annoying portmanteaus are universally loved by lazy journalists no matter where in the world you are. The republic would rise again!

At the beginning of the nineteenth century you'd find three words scrawled on the doors of abandoned houses throughout the United States: "Gone to Texas." The United States had experienced its first financial wobble in 1819, and Texas—still part of Mexico at this point—was seen by many as a better bet than staying put.[100] An independent Texas would come about as a direct result of this sudden mass migration. In fact, the republic had already briefly popped into existence (and then popped straight back out again) in 1813. Americans fighting the Spanish on behalf of Mexico decided to go it alone, only to be instantly crushed by the Spanish army. The revolution of 1835—this time against the much-despised Mexican leader Santa Anna—enjoyed more success. A brief war and the heroic last stand at the Alamo gave Texas the origin story it needed.

Niche businesses sprang up to cater to the new country. The Library of Congress contains an advert for Texan Universal Pills: "Prepared after a careful personal examination of the diseases incident to this climate, and with a particular reference to the health, comfort, and happiness of the Citizens of this Republic" (general directions include "keep up large evacuations to cleanse the system.") But shared diseases and regular bowel movements aren't enough to hang a country on, and Texas never truly established a national identity. Partly because from the very start the nation intended to join the United States. The republic was broke: it had inherited a million-dollar debt from the revolution, and the population was too cash-poor to pay much in the way of tax. They issued their own money, but with nothing to back it up it instantly lost

[100] This immigration would continue throughout the life of the state: in 1836 there were 30,000 whites, 5,000 black slaves, 3,470 Mexicans, and 14,200 Native Americans. By 1847, the numbers were: 103,000 whites, 39,000 black slaves, 295 free blacks, and nobody even bothered to count the Native Americans.

its value.[101] The Comanche still controlled great swathes of the country's supposed territory. That the republic lasted for even ten years was more down to the fact that many in the Union vehemently opposed Texas joining. It was "that valley of rascals," and the North feared that it would swell the power of a slave-owning South. Which could in turn start a terrible civil war. But luckily the naysayers were persuaded that was Project Fear talking.

None of this has stopped self-styled Texians from trying to keep the flame of independence alive. The extra hardcore ones don't even want to secede from the Union, because, as far as they're concerned, they never legally joined in the first place. They produce their own currency, have their own supposed court of law, and occasionally get raided by the FBI because neither of those things are very legal.[102]

---

[101] The republic failed to pay the £160 rent on its London embassy (a room above an off-licence) until 1986, when an unofficial delegation finally turned up to settle the bill.

[102] In 2003, the state of Texas passed a law obliging school children to salute the Texas "Lone Star" flag as well as Old Glory. It is probably best not to mention the whole West Florida thing.

THE CONGO FREE STATE
1885–1908

POPULATION: ESTIMATES VARY, BUT APPROXIMATELY 20 MILLION
    (AT THE START), 8 MILLION (BY THE END)
CAPITALS: VIVI, BOMA
LANGUAGES: FRENCH, DUTCH, AND OVER 200 INDIGENOUS
    LANGUAGES
CURRENCY: CONGO FREE STATE FRANC
CAUSE OF DEATH: TOO EVIL EVEN FOR TURN-OF-THE-CENTURY
    EUROPE TO STOMACH
TODAY: THE DEMOCRATIC REPUBLIC OF THE CONGO
///EAGLES.CLOCKING.DAILY

Lots of the countries in this book have misleading names, but
none are as totally wrong as "the Congo Free State." And
lots of the people in this book are terrible bastards, but none of
them are as irredeemably grim as Leopold II of Belgium.

His father—Leopold I—had interviewed for the position of king of Greece but turned it down and went with the Belgium vacancy instead. He almost instantly regretted taking the job, finding his kingdom boring and parochial. Thinking it might be fun to start an empire he began to eye up Texas but died before his colonial dreams could be fulfilled. Unfortunately for everyone, his son—an unattractive, arrogant teen who grew up to be an even worse adult—inherited his dad's expansionist streak. He briefly considered buying Sarawak off James Brooke (*see* page 20). Then somewhere more lucrative caught his eye.

The explorer Verney Lovett Cameron had recently completed a coast-to-coast journey across Africa and wrote a letter to *The Times* detailing his exploits. He told of a "magnificent and healthy country of unspeakable richness." Dollar signs flashed in Leopold's eyes. The immediate problem: he wasn't an absolute monarch. There were annoying issues like "public opinion" and "a government" to deal with—and neither of those had any interest in colonising Africa. But Leopold was well-connected and immensely rich, and that goes a long way when it comes to doing whatever you fancy.

The king set about convincing the world his ambitions towards the Congo were entirely philanthropic. He launched the International Association for the Exploration and Civilisation of Central Africa—effectively a cover story to keep other European powers from getting antsy. Phase Two of the plan was to employ distinguished explorer Henry Morton Stanley (of "Doctor Livingstone, I presume?" fame) to travel through the interior of the continent, "purchasing" millions of acres of land (illiterate tribal leaders marking a piece of paper with an "X" being deemed an important part of keeping this all above board). This wasn't being done on behalf of Belgium, Leopold made clear—it was a purely personal affair. His own private bit of magnanimous charity, helping out his fellow man.

The initial moneymaker was ivory (and he didn't skimp on this—by the 1890s most of the region's elephants were dead), but in the late 1880s John Dunlop invented the pneumatic tyre and even bigger dollar signs started floating in front of Leopold's eyes. He would become a rubber baron, and his "Free State" would become his personal dictatorial rubber plantation.[103] The Force Publique, a military made up of European officers and African soldiers, oversaw the districts where the impoverished Congolese were forced to work. While quelling the inevitable uprisings, and to prove they weren't wasting ammunition, the Force were required to cut off a hand of each of their victims and bring it back as a macabre receipt.

Nowhere was particularly enlightened at the turn of the century,[104] so it's a measure of how horrific Leopold's regime was that when word started to get out it caused a public outcry. A man called Edmund D. Morel, working at a shipping company in Liverpool, was one of the first whistleblowers. He studied the books of his employers and did a simple bit of detective work. The Congo Free State was exporting huge quantities of ivory and rubber. But all it seemed to be *importing* was a huge quantity of guns—no tradable goods to exchange with the populace. The only conclusion to be drawn: the locals weren't being paid, and this was a slave state on an industrial scale.

Morel set out to expose it, publishing a series of anonymous articles. The British government started an investigation. In a

---

[103] Leopold's smash-and-grab plan wasn't even intended to be sustainable—the rubber in the Congo came from vines rather than trees, which were destroyed in the process.

[104] Some context: as late as 1906, a Congolese man called Ota Benga was being exhibited in the Bronx Zoo's primate enclosure.

rare political misstep, Leopold reacted petulantly, calling the Brits hypocrites (not totally unfair, that) and improbably blaming Congo's rapid depopulation on sleeping sickness. Eventually his own embarrassed government took the Free State off his hands, though not before he'd received a handsome payoff. Upwards of 10 million had died by then. Leopold himself had never even bothered to set foot in the place.[105]

[105] After Leopold's death, Belgium embarked upon "the great forgetting." They did such a brilliant job of taking care of the Congo that by the time it won independence there were only a handful of Congolese graduates and not a single doctor, lawyer or engineer.

RUTHENIA (CARPATHO-UKRAINE)
15–16 MARCH 1939

POPULATION: 814,000
CAPITAL: KHUST
LANGUAGE: UKRAINIAN
CAUSE OF DEATH: HUNGARY
TODAY: PART OF UKRAINE
///BLIGHTED.SHARPENER.CHATTERBOX

The chemist Karl Ernst Claus liked to test the strength of acid by dipping his finger in it and touching it to his tongue. After managing to isolate the highly toxic compound osmium tetroxide, he described it as "tasting like pepper." Despite this approach to health and safety, Claus lived long enough to discover an entirely new element: ruthenium, number 44 in the periodic table, named after his motherland, Ruthenia.

As an independent country, Ruthenia lasted more than 15 minutes—but just barely, which is maybe appropriate given that the other famous person hailing from the Ruthenian diaspora is Andy Warhol. The term "Ruthenian" comes from the Rus' (same as the Russians, Belorussians and Ukrainians), which in turn probably comes from Old Norse. A group of Vikings once made their way across the Baltic, then on into the shadow of the Carpathian Mountains, where they settled down and became woodcutters—or at least that's a theory. There are a lot of probably-happened and thought-to-haves involved in piecing together the background of this part of the world. It's this same ethnic vagueness that makes the rest of the Balkans so unpredictable. But however they got there, and whoever they were, for 50 years the Ruthenians and "Ruthenia" were part of the Austro-Hungarian Empire. That formally kicked the bucket in 1918, at which point they found themselves in Czechoslovakia.

By 1938, Britain and France were fully committed to their brilliant "let's appease the fascists" strategy. They agreed that it would be fine if Hitler goose-stepped into Czechoslovakia, so long as he absolutely promised to call it a day and stop at that. At 5 A.M. on 15 March 1939, the Nazis seized the area that's now the Czech Republic, leaving the other big chunk of the country, Slovakia, to declare independence.

This put Ruthenia in a bind. They were cut off from Prague. They didn't much like the look of the Nazis. Stalin's Soviet Union didn't strike them as a fantastic option either. So, that same afternoon they decided to copy Slovakia and go it alone. A former maths teacher headed up the new government. In a remarkably efficient bit of country-building they'd already settled on an anthem and a flag before nightfall. Everyone went to bed a citizen of the new independent Ruthenian Republic of Carpatho-Ukraine. That's not where they woke up. In the early hours, the Hungarians invaded, spying the opportunity for a land grab (with a nod and a wink from an approving Hitler). The population had managed to find themselves under the rule of three different countries in 24 hours. One observer at the time recorded the slight farce of living through all this: "As soon as the troops had passed, a lawyer in the house opposite darted out and put a Hungarian name plate on his door. It was the fifth time he had changed it in the last twenty years, he said."

Even countries that only exist for a day leave a legacy. Today, some Ruthenians are once again pressing for independence—though to what extent this is a genuine desire for self-determination and to what extent it's Putin up to his old tricks, quietly stirring the nationalism pot to destabilise Ukraine, is anyone's guess (but yes, it's definitely at least partly Putin).

PEOPLE'S REPUBLIC OF TANNU TUVA
1921–44

POPULATION: 95,000
CAPITAL: KYZYL
LANGUAGES: TUVAN, RUSSIAN, MONGOLIAN
CURRENCY: TUVAN AKSA
CAUSE OF DEATH: STALIN
TODAY: PART OF RUSSIA
///SNEEZED.PILOTS.SHOWER

For Nobel Prize-winning physicist/amateur bongo player Richard Feynman, Tuva represented the platonic ideal of a Mysterious Lost Nation. A blob in the middle of Asia only found on old globes, with distinctive triangular and diamond-shaped stamps only found in old stamp albums, a pervasive lack of information about the ex-country had intrigued him since he was a kid. He resolved to pay it a visit.

To add to its appeal, Tuva was near impossible to get to, partly because of the remote location—it's not really on the way to anywhere—and partly because the Cold War was in full swing. You couldn't simply hop on a plane and turn up. But the main thing that attracted Feynman was the fact that the name of the capital, Kyzyl, didn't contain any vowels, which is a good enough reason to want to visit a place.[106] Though in case the lack of vowels wasn't enough of a tourist draw, the city also claimed to lie at the exact geographical centre of Asia, which it marked with a monument. There are a lot of ways you can mathematically argue to be the centre of an irregularly shaped landmass, so China has also staked a claim—700 miles to the southwest. Their monument is slightly taller.[107]

The other thing Tuva has going for it is throat singing, which is either an attraction (the effect of one person singing in two distinctive "voices" simultaneously is genuinely incredible) or a great reason not to visit (it does sound a *lot* like bagpipes). Anthropologists suggest the practice arose because of the geography: the deep persistent drone of throat singing travels for miles over vast open plains. Aside from yurts and yaks, there isn't anything much to interrupt it.

Tuva had been part of Mongolia before the Russians arrived in 1912. The Bolshevik revolution saw it occupied first by the Red Army, then the Chinese army. By 1921 a new government had proclaimed the independent Tuvan People's Republic. The increasingly Soviet-influenced rulers tried to stamp out Buddhism, with some success, and also the nomadic lifestyle, with almost no success at all. When Tuva was later swallowed

---

[106] Bit Anglocentric though (Turkish speakers would know that Kyzyl means "red," it's not that exotic).

[107] There was already a village located at the rival Chinese centre-of-Asia geographical point, so the government knocked it down and moved it less than a mile away in order to build their monument.

by the USSR, officially it was because the Tuvan people voluntarily requested to join the glorious union—and absolutely not because the huge load of uranium deposited in the mountains suddenly looked a lot more interesting to Stalin in 1944.[108]

Feynman and the society he set up—the Friends of Tuva—spent years trying to arrange a visit, battling impenetrable Soviet bureaucracy. In the end, the letter from the Russian tourist department granting Feynman permission finally arrived . . . two days after he had died.

[108] Partly thanks to Feynman's youthful work on the Manhattan Project, irony fans.

# The Republic of Salò
## 1943–45

CAPITAL: SALÒ (THOUGH OFFICIALLY ROME)
CURRENCY: ITALIAN LIRA
CAUSE OF DEATH: PUPPET OF A 1,000-YEAR REICH THAT DIDN'T
    LAST A DECADE
TODAY: NORTHERN ITALY
///REBUILT.FLUORINE.HYPOCRITE

On 25 July 1943, Benito Mussolini turned up for a meeting with the Italian king, Victor Emmanuel III. Usually the king would listen politely as the journalist-turned-fascist-strongman gave his pompous report. This time, Mussolini found himself interrupted. The king informed him that the war was lost, morale had collapsed, and he was now the most hated man in Italy. The police bundled Il Duce into an ambulance and put him under house arrest.

SALÒ

ITALIAN SOCIAL REPUBLIC

The
REPUBLIC
of
SALÒ

Reaction in the country was instant: some rejoiced, some screamed betrayal. Most were just tired of a terrible war and hopeful that this would see the end of it. But the government dithered, fearful of both sides. When Italy finally announced an armistice, the new prime minister succinctly summed up the situation at a meeting of his cabinet. *"Siamo fottuti,"* he declared. We are *screwed.*

The already-shattered army waited for orders, and none came. In the south, in places like Naples—always up for a fight—a fierce resistance drove the Nazis out. But, in the north, it was a different story: here the Germans swept through the country, taking prisoner a million Italians in the process. They dug in across the Apennine mountain range, cutting Italy in two. SS commandos busted Mussolini out of the ski resort where he was being held captive. Benito was unexpectedly back in charge of a new "republic."

All countries rely on belief, or at least a suspension of disbelief. They need a reason to exist based on a common history or people or language or adversary—or, most usually, some poorly thought-out mix of all of those. Italy had spent the last two decades taking itself much too seriously, not the first or last nation to come unstuck getting high on its own mythology. Mussolini had been an expert at invoking the glories of Garibaldi and the Roman Empire to stoke nationalist pride. Which is what he half-heartedly attempted again with the Republic of Salò. But it's hard to convince yourself or anyone else that you're a squat reincarnation of Caesar in a nice felt hat, when you take all your orders from a shouty Austrian a few hundred miles away.

The puppet state would have been embarrassing if it weren't also so grim. There was a daily shortage of rations. Gas and electricity supplies were near non-existent. Kids plaintively scrawled the Italian word for "bread" on walls, and all the cats ominously disappeared. Mussolini grew bitter and depressed. On meeting him, one conscript reported in his diary: "He is ugly: his face is spotted with the purple blotches of someone with liver disorder. He is deflated, thin."[109] The man who invented topless machismo-based photo ops was long gone.

When the Allies broke through the fortified defensive line of the Apennines, huge numbers tried to escape north. The Germans were allowed to leave, but not the Italians. Mussolini wrote a touching letter to his wife and then tried to do a runner with his mistress. Partisans found him hiding under a blanket in the corner of a lorry, dressed in a German soldier's coat. This is not enough of a disguise if you've had your face stuck up on gigantic banners for a couple of decades. They shot him with a sub-machine gun and hung his corpse from a petrol station. Which makes Mussolini one of the rare monsters in this book who actually received a comeuppance.[110]

Today, Mussolini's tomb gets around a hundred thousand adoring visitors a year.

---

[109] As recounted in *Fascist Voices* (Christopher Duggan)

[110] Alessandra Mussolini, a member of the European Parliament, recently threatened to sue anyone writing disrespectful comments about her disastrous, possibly syphilitic grandfather.

## THE GERMAN DEMOCRATIC REPUBLIC
### 1949–90

POPULATION: 16 MILLION (IN 1990)
CAPITAL: EAST BERLIN
LANGUAGE: GERMAN
CURRENCY: EAST GERMAN MARK
CAUSE OF DEATH: NOT A POP CONCERT
TODAY: PART OF GERMANY
///ANIMATED.CAGE.KITE

Even today, two diametrically opposed and irreconcilable belief systems keep butting up against each other: those that think it was David Bowie who brought about the fall of the Berlin Wall, and those who swear it was David Hasselhoff. It's fair to say that neither of these points of view tell the entire story.

On the night of 12 August 1961, soldiers built what was officially known as an "anti-fascist protection rampart," and Berlin woke up to find itself cut in two. The non-democratic, non-republic German Democratic Republic (GDR) had come into being 12 years before, but it had been bleeding at a catastrophic rate: by the time the wall went up, 3.5 million people—a full 20 per cent of the population—had fled to the west.

The wall didn't stop East Berliners trying to get out, but it staunched the flow. In one of the bureaucratic nonsenses that would become commonplace in the GDR, applying to leave was still considered legal, but you'd automatically be suspected of a *Hetzschrift*—thinking ill of the republic—and that was definitely a crime. The Germans soon got used to this type of doublethink. Everything in the east fell under the watchful eyes of the Stasi, and with 97,000 employees—plus a network of almost 200,000 informers—they had a *lot* of eyes.[111] They'd censor your books and listen to your phone calls and check the direction of your TV aerial to make sure you were watching wholesome shows like *Treffpunkt Flughafen* (a drama set on the GDR's state airline, Interflug) rather than decadent Western efforts (*Dallas* became super popular after the authorities loosened up a little).

Escape might have been tricky, but there was another—officially sanctioned—way out, which is partly how the GDR managed to survive. A system developed in which the east would voluntarily send dissidents to the west. The benefit was twofold: it earned the regime hard cash (West Germany would pay a set amount for each citizen), and it acted as a release valve to keep political pressure from building up—those most likely to ferment unrest could simply be exported to where they'd do no harm.

When Mikhail Gorbachev embarked upon *glasnost* in the

[111] Old GDR joke: why do Stasi work together in groups of three? You need one who can read, one who can write and one to keep an eye on two intellectuals.

1980s and it became apparent that the Stasi could no longer rely on the threat of Russian tanks as a backup, the German Democratic Republic's days were numbered, regardless of whether the lyrics to either "Heroes" (Bowie) or "Looking for Freedom" (Hasselhoff) were wafting across from the other side of the wall. The end was a confused mess: East Germany's Politbüro announced a relaxation of the travel ban. Asked when this would take effect, hapless schmuck Günter Schabowski (charged with telling the press but not present at the meeting the plan had been thrashed out in) scratched his head, shrugged, and said: "Immediately?" The people swarmed over the wall. Caught off guard by this, the Stasi desperately ran out to buy some Western shredders, because their crappy Soviet ones had already broken down, and they realised they had the mother of all cover-up jobs to try to get through.

Today, *Ostalgie* (combining the German words for "east" and "nostalgia") has become the term for the semi-wistful attachment people have for their former lives in the GDR. The east was pervasive alcoholism, queues round the block for bananas, the legal requirement for pop music to be sung in German, 3 million unreliable Trabants, desperate adverts urging people to "eat another egg" (after an overproduction of poultry), but it was also a completely socialised public health-care system and an arguably more progressive view of women than you'd find in West Germany at the time.[112] Plus, there were all those rules to follow, and a lot of people find comfort in having rules, even if the rules are stupid and sometimes evil.

[112] The country developed its own covert slang, as in "Vitamin B"—B for *Beziehungen*, meaning "connections"—the term for smuggled goods from the west. A large percentage of the GDR's population made their own clothes rather than rely on the very lumpen official offerings.

# BOPHUTHATSWANA
## 1977–94

POPULATION: CIRCA 1.5 MILLION
CAPITAL: MMABATHO
LANGUAGES: TSWANA, ENGLISH, AFRIKAANS
CURRENCY: SOUTH AFRICAN RAND. TWO "BOPHUTHATSWANAN"
   COINS, THE LOWE AND THE NKWE, WERE MADE FOR PUBLIC-
   ITY PURPOSES AND NEVER GOT PAST THE PROOF STAGE
CAUSE OF DEATH: IT WASN'T FOOLING ANYBODY
TODAY: PART OF SOUTH AFRICA
///CUCUMBER.BLEND.QUITE

If you are looking at this map and thinking "that's a funny shape for a country, nation states don't tend to be a load of random separate blobs," you would have a good point. Bophuthatswana was one of the Bantustans, a racist 1970s sequel to Maryland in Africa (see page 192).

Maryland had been an attempt to dump an unwanted black population on another continent, something South Africa's white apartheid government couldn't do. For a start, there wasn't much of the globe still up for grabs. But also: the economy depended on the very people they wanted rid of. So South Africa came up with a weasel solution, one that would disenfranchise all those citizens they didn't want to give the vote to, but without messing up their ability to do hard labour. It was evil and ingenious: the "repatriation" of the people to their "original" tribal homelands. Who could object to this generous offer of self-determination?[113]

The shapes ended up as weird as they were from simple greed: the government wasn't about to let these new "countries" have any land that might actually be good for something, because the whole point was that the inhabitants would be forced to commute back to South Africa to earn a wage. When a load of titanium was discovered after the map of "self-governing entity" KwaZulu had already been drawn, a narrow strip was simply lopped off it and declared "development land." As a result of this geographical gerrymandering, if you wanted to travel through Bophuthatswana (the second Bantustan declared independent) you'd have to go through passport control a ridiculous dozen times. Nobody wants that many Toblerones. (Note: there were no Toblerones, or money to buy Toblerones with.)

A bonus for the whites: the under-resourced new "nations" could argue with each other over their crappy territories rather than target the real problem. Double bonus: once issued with an ID card informing them of their new nationalities, the pop-

---

[113] The Nazis came up with a similar scheme when they were drawing up plans for the future conquest of Africa, though semi-inevitably it was the British who first mooted the idea.

ulace lost their pension rights and the "unproductive" members of society (mostly women and children) were suddenly off the government's books.[114]

In Bophuthatswana, a new capital city was built. It included a parliament building, a luxury hotel, a garage selling "farm fresh petrol," a half-finished stadium and virtually nothing else. The authorities had put the bare minimum of effort into making it seem like a real place. To celebrate "independence," field guns fired a presidential salute, causing all the nearby cows to charge away in a panic, and a gymnastics team—boycotted by all the good gymnasts—gave a clumsy performance. Later, in a political pantomime designed to confer legitimacy, one of the Bantustans cut off diplomatic relations with South Africa. "We can't be a South African puppet if we're angry with them, can we?" went the extremely see-through ruse.[115]

With the exceptions of Barclays bank and a bunch of English cricketers, the rest of the world wasn't swallowing it. Despite plenty of wining and dining from ambassadors, nobody agreed to recognise the Bantustans diplomatically. South Africa's isolation grew and when a triumphant Nelson Mandela finally swept to victory in 1994, the fake countries were once again wiped from the map. Nobody mourned their passing.

---

[114] Another neat trick: when an awkward question was asked in the South African parliament about an issue like healthcare in one of the poorer areas, the minister in charge could now say, "Ah, that is a matter for the national government of X, not something I can answer."

[115] There were ten Bantustans in total, six "self-governing entities" and four "fully independent states."

REPUBLIC OF CRIMEA
17–18 MARCH 2014

POPULATION: CIRCA 2 MILLION
CAPITAL: SIMFEROPOL
LANGUAGES: RUSSIAN, UKRAINIAN, CRIMEAN TARTAR
CURRENCY: RUSSIAN RUBLE, UKRAINIAN HRYVNIA
CAUSE OF DEATH: THE COMPARATIVELY NICE WEATHER
TODAY: A (DISPUTED) PART OF RUSSIA
///MERE.CRAB.JUGGLED

The problem with being a Bold Man of Action like Vladimir Putin is that there are only so many creatures you can wrestle with your shirt off/migrating geese you can lead back home in your micro-glider/ancient urns you can find on your impromptu and very legitimate underwater archaeological dives. When the photo ops run dry you've got one option left, the predictable choice of all good despots: take over Crimea.

For hundreds of years, Crimea has found itself in a constant state of getting conquered and re-conquered. Surrounded by a sea that can burst into flames during a thunderstorm—dead vegetation from the last ice age has created a barren zone 90 metres down from which noxious flammable gas occasionally bubbles up—the Crimean peninsula also lies on one of those geopolitical fault lines that means it's doomed to have an exhausting time of it.

According to Herodotus, the first settlers were the Cimmerians, who were such an incredibly proud people they opted for mass suicide when invaded by the Scythians.[116] After the Scythians came the Greeks, then the Taurians, the Goths, the Kipchaks, the Alans,[117] the Rus," the Khazars, the Armenians, the Mongols and the Genoese. For the Russian tsars, Crimea had represented a relaxing holiday home, a rare piece of the empire where your face wouldn't freeze off if you tried to go for a swim.

Years later, the distant twisted memory of one of those early eras—the Ostrogothic Kingdom—would be the basis for a new Gothia; a brief, evil regime set up by the Nazis during World War II that led to the deaths of thousands. That was followed by Stalin, who set about deporting the mainly Tartar population to gulags.[118] The whole place was then gifted to Ukraine by the Soviets as a showy anniversary present—Nikita Khrushchev mistakenly believing it went paper, cotton, Crimea. This didn't mean all that much though, seeing as

---

[116] As ever, even though the peninsula is one of the places Herodotus visited rather than just imagined from the comfort of his couch, he is not a *totally* reliable source.

[117] The Alans weren't some men all called Alan; they were Iranian nomads.

[118] The Putin-baiting, Ukrainian winner of the 2016 Eurovision song contest was about Stalin's deportation of the Tartars from Crimea.

Ukraine was firmly part of the USSR—a situation nobody saw changing anytime soon.

But that empire crumbled too, like they do.[119] When Ukraine started its political drift towards the West, the peninsula's fate became semi-inevitable. The big problem for Russia was that Sevastopol is one of the only warm water ports it had access to and there was no way a Bold Man of Action was going to see that slip away under his watch.

On 16 March 2014, Crimea held a referendum to proclaim independence, albeit a brief and very unconvincing independence of one single day prior to falling back into Russia's arms. And while that referendum was certainly a bit suspect, the situation is (slightly) more complicated than a rapacious Putin flat-out stealing some territory: after Stalin's decimation of the Tartars, much of the now largely Russian population on the peninsula were simply more sympathetic to throwing their lot in with the motherland. The West made a lot of unhappy noises on behalf of Ukraine, and were ultimately pretty happy not to be forced to intervene. Russia has the pipelines and a lot of Europe quite likes being able to heat their homes in winter. But it would be a bad bet to assume that this is the last time Crimea finds itself under new ownership.

---

[119] Crimea also had a flirtation with independence in 1992, when in the wake of the Soviet Union's collapse it separated from Ukraine for just over an entire week.

# Yugoslavia
## 1918–41, 1945–92

POPULATION: 23 MILLION (BY 1991)
CAPITAL: BELGRADE
LANGUAGES: SERBO-CROATIAN, MACEDONIAN, SLOVENE
CURRENCY: DINAR
CAUSE OF DEATH: NOBODY THOUGHT THEY WERE FROM YUGOSLAVIA
TODAY: BOSNIA AND HERZEGOVINA, CROATIA, KOSOVO, MONTENEGRO, NORTH MACEDONIA, SERBIA, SLOVENIA
///KOALA.PLOTTING.DRAMATIC

In 1989, a band called Riva won the Eurovision Song Contest with the numbingly dull "Rock Me." This meant Yugoslavia got to be hosts the following year. By the time 1990 rolled around, things were looking shaky. The Croatians were unimpressed by the Serbian singer chosen to represent them. The Serbs rolled their eyes at what they regarded as inept Croatian staging. The song came seventh.

# YUGOSLAVIA

SLOVENIA
LJUBLJANA    ZAGREB
CROATIA
VOJVODINA
NOVI SAD
BOSNIA AND
HERZEGOVINA
BELGRADE
SARAJEVO
SERBIA
MONTENEGRO    PRISTINA
PODGORICA    KOSOVO
SKOPJE
MACEDONIA

The year after that, the Yugoslav entry came second to last. The year after *that* the country didn't exist, at least not in the same form that had so improbably been turning up for the previous three decades. The question was how it had ever managed to last that long.

The answer can be summed up as: Tito. The new Kingdom of Yugoslavia,[120] barely out of its bubble wrap, first fell apart in World War II. Croatia enthusiastically hooked up with the Axis powers. So enthusiastically in fact, that the Nazis found the Croat massacres of the Serbs a bit hard to stomach (compared to their own, much neater genocides). The Serbian nationalist Chetniks, with their skull-and-crossbones flag, matched their neighbour's violent zeal, atrocity for atrocity. Tito's Communist partisans were the third strand of a messy conflict, and the ones who came out on top. Mutual war crimes aren't the *most* solid basis for a nation, but over the next 30 years Tito managed to wodge everything back together, partly through sheer force of personality.

He was the communist who liked to eat off solid gold plates. The seventh of fifteen children, his real genius was being able to adjust. He juggled and re-juggled the conflicting interests of the populace. Most significantly, he dared to disagree with Stalin. Stalin took being disagreed with in the exact way you would imagine: not well. After Yugoslavia went off on its own non-Soviet, non-capitalist "third way," Tito had to send a letter to the Russian leader politely requesting that he stop trying to have him assassinated.[121]

---

[120] Yugoslavia emerged as more than just a concept in 1918, though at first it was called "the Kingdom of Serbs, Croats and Slovenes." This catchy name gives a clue as to the fact this wasn't a country entirely dreamed up by the locals, but by Woodrow Wilson's hopeful new League of Nations as an attempt to make some sense of the existing Balkan states, at that point regarded as an international headache.

[121] Tito's letter, supposedly found among Stalin's papers after his death, said: "Stop sending people to kill me. If you don't stop I'll send one to Moscow, and I won't have to send a second."

The economy grew, literacy rates soared, Yugoslavia seemed to prosper under Tito. Especially Tito himself, who had 32 official residences, a fancy yacht and his own private zoo. But, under the surface, the country was racking up crippling deficits. Everyone suspected things would go south again without the unifying figure of the man in charge. The hope was that he would somehow live forever.

He died on 4 May 1980 at 3:05 P.M. The meaningless and slightly desperate catchphrase adopted by the Communists in the aftermath of his death—"After Tito—Tito!"—suggests they knew the problem they were facing. The country limped on but the centrifugal forces of nationalism span faster. When the rebranded Communists' unintentionally funny new slogan—"This time we mean it!"—failed to impress, nationalists swept to power in Croatia. Meanwhile Serbia, seeing itself as the dutiful grown-up holding the federation together, was now under the sway of the murderous Slobodan Milošević. When multi-ethnic Bosnia declared independence in 1992, the whole place blew up into a predictably horrific war.

It's common to say that Yugoslavia never made sense as a country,[122] which is true, but it's also true that the forces that ripped it apart never made much sense either. Religious differences pretended to be national ones. The Croats thought the Serbs made their coffee wrong; the Serbs thought the Croats were too flashy by half. Both thought the Slovenes were only interested in money. The history of "ethnic origins" in Europe is an impossibly complicated subject full of holes and conjecture; archaeologists and historians are left scratching their heads. The Yugoslav population, like most populations, based their identity and mutual mistrust on . . . nothing very much. But ludicrous little details can be enough to bring a nation down; it doesn't *always* have to be Napoleon.

---

[122] In 1991, only 6 per cent of the population identified as "Yugoslavian."

# FLAGS
## "FLAGS AREN'T IMPORTANT, YOU CAN'T EAT A FLAG."

So said the chief minister of the KwaZulu Bantustan, explaining why his fake country didn't have one.[123] He was wrong. If Monsieur Mangetout could eat an entire aeroplane, then you could certainly eat a flag so long as you put your mind to it. But also: obviously flags are important; people take almost nothing else as seriously as they take flags, even the ones from extinct countries. The Confederate States of America hasn't been a thing for a century and a half, but that doesn't stop cowardly Nazis (in those parts of Europe where the swastika is banned) from using the Confederate flag as a coded bumper sticker. The Taiwanese flag emoji noticeably fails to appear on Chinese iPhones. For a brief time, if you flew the flag of Wales at the Eurovision song contest, they'd have kicked you out.

Another reason that flags are important: there is a strong argument to be made that a full 90 per cent of the reason people start countries in the first place is because they want an excuse to get into flag design. How else to explain the number of supposedly busy leaders who found the time to personally sit down and sketch something out themselves? Or the fact that several nations got around to the flag stuff even before they sorted out more pressing matters, like a government?

[123] Two days after saying that flags weren't important and that it wouldn't have a flag, KwaZulu had a flag.

But not all flags are created equal, so here are the Top Five Deceased National Flags:

**The Principality of Elba**: Designed by Napoleon himself en route to his exile, who took the old flag and added some bees, correctly following the twin principles that 1) any creature on a flag automatically improves it and 2) everyone likes bees. If he hadn't already had his conquering-the-world hobby, Napoleon would have made an excellent full-time flag designer. Supposedly the bees represented "power and immortality." Bees are not immortal—they live for about 120 days and die if they have sex—so it's safe to say Napoleon wasn't a bee expert.

**The Kingdom of Corsica**: A legitimately clever bit of rejigging by the Corsican rebels. Like Napoleon, they tweaked the old emblem—in their case it showed a blindfolded slave, which they redrew with the blindfold now worn as a bandana to demonstrate their liberation from the Genoese.

**The People's Republic of Tannu Tuva**: A good colour scheme, a map of the country, plus a man with a lance on a flying horse. While the Kingdom of Sikkim simplified its flag because it was felt the old version was too hard to draw, Tuva fully committed to being Overly Busy, which is a relief in a world of quite boring flags that could do with more going on.

**The Free State of Fiume:** Like his hero Napoleon, D'Annunzio took a hands-on approach and designed his own flag. A snake eating its own tail! The constellation of Orion (possibly a homage to his friends in the IRA)! An unusual vertical design to make it extra-fascist! The up-in-your-face "Who is against us?" motto! D'Annunzio can't be accused of holding back, at any rate.

**The Republic of Formosa:** The happiest face on any flag. They should commission a Netflix series about the Formosa tiger having adventures. Along with his pals the Dahomey crown-wearing elephant and the Perloja religious bison.

Y ou've got a lot of choices to make when trying to settle on your country's anthem. "Indistinguishable pompous dirge" is the most popular option. "Upbeat to the point of insanity" is a close second. For hardcore masochists, the Greek anthem goes on for 158 verses. Japan gets it done in four lines. A handful of places wisely settle for instrumentals, to save on awkward Olympic podium miming issues.

Approaches taken by deceased nations:

### EMO
The Kingdom of Corsica hid behind a fringe and stomped up the stairs to its room and wanted you to know that it was very dark and serious and didn't listen to that normcore pop fluff other countries were into:

*Towards you sighs and moans*
*Our distressed heart*
*In a sea of pain*
*And bitterness.*
*In a sea of pain*
*And bitterness.*

It goes on repeating that last part, in case you've not yet got a handle on how miserable they were.

### BOASTFUL

The semi-comical anthem written for Orélie-Antoine de Tounen's Araucanía took a Trumpian approach to self-deprecating understatement:

*Oh great Orélie, Lord of the Mapuches.*
*You are famous without equal*
*Orélie, to your honour fifty pretty girls will dance the*
*Malumbo.*

FIFTY.

### BOASTFUL YET ALSO UNDERWHELMING

Tuva's anthem (taken from an old folk song) made a big deal of having "nine different animals," which is not that many animals. In a touchingly optimistic but misguided coda, it also talks about how if they feed the nine different animals, they'll get rich.

### LAZY

When the Soviet Union died, Russia kept the tune and simply changed the lyrics to something a bit less Soviet. Meanwhile, Neutral Moresnet just swapped out the words to "Little Christmas Tree" (and did it in Esperanto, of course).

### TARDY

Yugoslavia didn't get around to adopting an anthem for ages, so the popular song "Hey, Slavs" became the unofficial one. In 1988, after 40 years, they finally decided to formally make "Hey, Slavs" their anthem, moments before the country collapsed. The lesson from this is: nail down your anthem early.

SELECT BIBLIOGRAPHY


Ackroyd, Peter. *Venice: Pure City* (Chatto & Windus, 2009).

Alpern, Stanley B. *Amazons of Black Sparta: The Women Warriors of Dahomey* (C Hurst & Co Publishers Ltd, 2011).

Applebaum, Anne. *Between East and West: Across the Borderlands of Europe* (Pantheon, 1994).

Barley, Nigel. *White Rajah: A Biography of Sir James Brooke* (Abacus, 2003).

Cronin, Vincent. *Napoleon* (HarperCollins, 1995).

Davis, Richard Harding. *Real Soldiers of Fortune* (Cornell University Library, 1907).

Diamond, Jared M. *Collapse: How Societies Choose to Fail or Survive* (Allen Lane, 2005).

Duara, Prasenjit. *Sovereignty and Authenticity: Manchukuo and the East Asian Modern* (Roman & Littlefield, 2003).

Duff, Andrew. *Sikkim: Requiem for a Himalayan Kingdom* (Birlinn Ltd, 2015).

Eade, Philip. *Sylvia, Queen of the Headhunters: An Outrageous Englishwoman and Her Lost Kingdom* (Weidenfeld & Nicolson, 2007).

Ewans, Martin. *European Atrocity, African Catastrophe: Leopold II, the Congo Free State and its Aftermath* (Curzon Press, 2002).

Finlayson, Iain. *Tangier: City of the Dream* (Bloomsbury Academic, 2015).

Funder, Anna. *Stasiland: Stories from Beyond the Berlin Wall* (Granta, 2011).

Gasper, Julia. *Theodore von Neuhoff, King of Corsica: The Man Behind the Legend* (University of Delaware Press, 2013).

Hall, Brian. *The Impossible Country: Journey Through the Last Days of Yugoslavia* (Penguin, 1994).

Hall, Richard L. *On Afric's Shore: A History of Maryland in Liberia, 1834–1857* (Maryland Historical Society, 2003).

Hughes-Hallett, Lucy. *The Pike: Gabriele d'Annunzio, Poet, Seducer and Preacher of War* (4th Estate, 2013).

Hwang, Kyung Moon. *A History of Korea* (Palgrave Macmillan, 2010).

Jampol, Justinian. *Beyond the Wall: Art and Artifacts from the GDR* (Taschen, 2014).

Jasanoff, Maya. *Liberty's Exiles: The Loss of America and the Remaking of the British Empire* (HarperPress, 2011).

Johnson, Charles. *The History of the Pyrates, Volume 2* (Charles Rivington, 1726).

Leighton, Ralph. *Tuva or Bust! Richard Feynman's Last Journey* (Viking, 1992).

Lovric, Michael. *Venice: Tales of the City* (Abacus, 2005). MacGregor, Neil. *Germany: Memories of a Nation* (Penguin, 2014).

McIntosh, Christopher. *The Swan King: Ludwig II of Bavaria* (Tauris Parke Paperbacks, 1997).

McLynn, Frank. *Genghis Khan: The Man Who Conquered the World* (Da Capo Press, 2015).

Pence, Katherine. *Socialist Modern: East German Everyday Culture and Politics* (The University of Michigan Press, 2008).

Phillipson, D.W. *Ancient Ethiopia: Aksum, Its Predecessors and Successors* (British Museum Press, 1998).

Prebble, John. *The Darien Disaster* (Pimlico, 2002). Roy, Denny. *Taiwan: A Political History* (Cornell University Press, 2003).

Sinclair, David. *The Land That Never Was: Sir Gregor MacGregor and the Most Audacious Fraud in History* (Da Capo Press, 2004).

Spence, Jonathan. *God's Chinese Son* (HarperCollins, 1996).

West, Richard. *Tito and the Rise and Fall of Yugoslavia* (Carroll & Graf, 1995).

Wilson, Sandra. *The Manchurian Crisis and Japanese Society 1931–33* (Routledge, 2002).

Wright, James Leitch. *William Augustus Bowles, Director General of the Creek Nation* (University of Georgia Press, 1967).

ACKNOWLEDGEMENTS

Important disclaimer: because of the pandemic, I've never met most of the people who helped put this book together. They might be terrible in real life.

EDITORIAL
Publisher / Editor: Kent Carroll
Assistant Editor: Raonaid Ryn
Editorial Assistant: Cliff Robbins
Proofreader: Nora Nussbaum

DESIGN
Illustrator: Joy Gosney
Cover Designer: Ellie Game / Emanuele Ragnisco

PRODUCTION
Production Manager: Leonella Basiglini
Production Assistant: Dafne Martino
Typesetter: Grafica Punto Print

MARKETING
Director of Sales & Marketing: Kathy Wiess
Sales & Marketing Assistant: Kristi Bontrager

PUBLICITY
Publicist: Tatiana Radujkovic

RIGHTS
Contracts Manager: Giulia Cuomo
Foreign Rights Manager: Emanuela Anechoum

A special thanks to Claire Conrad, who got me to write this in the first place; Helen Garnons-Williams, for saving it from development hell; Tom Espley, for being a really great A level history teacher; the staff at the British Library; and, as always, mum.